The Imputation of the Active Obedience of Christ in the Westminster Standards

Explorations in
Reformed Confessional Theology

Editors
Daniel R. Hyde and Dan Borvan

The Imputation of the Active Obedience of Christ in the Westminster Standards

Alan D. Strange

REFORMATION HERITAGE BOOKS
Grand Rapids, Michigan

Reformation Heritage Books
2965 Leonard St. NE
Grand Rapids, MI 49525
616-977-0889
orders@heritagebooks.org
www.heritagebooks.org

Printed in the United States of America
19 20 21 22 23/10 9 8 7 6 5 4 3 2 1

Library of Congress Cataloging-in-Publication Data

Names: Strange, Alan D., author.
Title: The imputation of the active obedience of Christ in the Westminster
    standards / Alan D. Strange.
Description: Grand Rapids, Michigan : Reformation Heritage Books, 2019. |
    Series: Explorations in reformed confessional theology | Includes
    bibliographical references and index. | Summary: "A survey of the textual,
    historical, theological, and pastoral issues related to the doctrine of the
    imputation of Christ's active obedience found in the Westminster
    Standards"—Provided by publisher.
Identifiers: LCCN 2019031075 (print) | LCCN 2019031076 (ebook) | ISBN
    9781601787149 (paperback) | ISBN 9781601787156 (epub)
Subjects: LCSH: Justification (Christian theology)—History of doctrines—
    17th century. | Obedience—Religious aspects—Christianity—History of
    doctrines—17th century. | Westminster Confession of Faith.
Classification: LCC BT764.3 .S77 2019 (print) | LCC BT764.3 (ebook) |
    DDC 234/.6—dc23
LC record available at https://lccn.loc.gov/2019031075
LC ebook record available at https://lccn.loc.gov/2019031076

For additional Reformed literature, request a free book list from Reformation Heritage Books at the above regular or e-mail address.

Contents

Series Preface

The creeds of the ancient church and the doctrinal standards of the sixteenth- and seventeenth-century Reformed churches are rich theological documents. They summarize the essential teachings of Scripture, express biblical doctrines in meaningful and memorable ways, and offer pastoral guidance for the heads and hearts of God's people. Nevertheless, when twenty-first-century readers pick up these documents, certain points may be found confusing, misunderstood, or irrelevant for the church.

The Exploration in Reformed Confessional Theology series intends to clarify some of these confessional issues from four vantage points. First, it views confessional issues from the *textual* vantage point, exploring such things as variants, textual development, and the development of language within the documents themselves as well as within the context in which these documents were written. Second, this series views confessional issues from the *historical* vantage point, exploring social history and the history of ideas that shed light upon these issues. Third, this series views confessional issues from the *theological* vantage point, exploring the issues of intra- and inter-confessional theology both in the days these documents were written as well as in our day. Fourth, this series views confessional issues from the *pastoral* vantage point, exploring the pressing pastoral needs of certain doctrines and the implications of any issues that cause difficulty in the confessions.

In exploring our vast and deep heritage in such a way, our ultimate goal is to "walk worthy of the Lord unto all pleasing, being fruitful in every good work, and increasing in the knowledge of God" (Col. 1:10).

Author's Preface

"I'm so thankful for the active obedience of Christ. No hope without it." These are the heralded dying words of J. Gresham Machen (1881–1937), one of the premier confessional Presbyterian theologians of the twentieth century, sent in a final telegram to his colleague at Westminster Theological Seminary, Professor John Murray (1898–1975). What thrilled him, as he reflected on recent discussions with Murray and a sermon on the radio Machen himself had given on the subject, was that Christ had fulfilled the law for His own: in His passive obedience, He not only suffered the wrath of God due us as lawbreakers but, in His active obedience, also kept the whole law for us.[1] Jesus not only died *for us* but lived *for us*, in our place.

It must have been no small comfort to the perishing defender of the faith that his hope was not in anything

---

1. Ned B. Stonehouse, *J. Gresham Machen: A Biographical Memoir* (1954; repr., Willow Grove, Pa.: Committee for the Historian of the Orthodox Presbyterian Church, 2004), 450–51. See also J. Gresham Machen, "Active Obedience of Christ," in *God Transcendent and Other Selected Sermons* (Grand Rapids: Eerdmans, 1949), 172–80.

that he had done, or could ever do, but only and entirely in what Christ had done for him in perfectly obeying the law in his place. Some have alleged that Christ's death for us gets us everything we need. In other words, although Christ died in our place, it was not necessary for Him to live in our place.[2] Christ's death indeed removes the debt of sin, but it is His active obedience accounted (or imputed) to us that gives us the perfect righteousness we need. We have a need not only for our sin to be paid for but also for the law to be kept for us positively.[3]

Some treat the requirement that sin's penalty be paid (as done in the imputation of Christ's passive obedience) and that the law's demands be fulfilled (as done in the imputation of Christ's active obedience) as a foreign idea, but it is common in our experience: we penalize a young person who fails to clean his room when he is told, and even after censuring him, we still require him to clean it. Adam, as covenant head of the human race, was required to keep the law perfectly and to pay the penalty for transgressing it. Christ came as the last Adam, the federal head of His elect, to pay the price of sin in His own body. He also perfectly obeyed the covenant that Adam failed to obey, taking the penalty for doing what Adam failed to do and actually rendering for us the obedience that Adam was bound to yield.[4]

---

2. See especially chaps. 1–3 and 7.

3. See chap. 1, notes 17 and 20.

4. Some have argued from passages like Hebrews 10:5–7 (citing Ps. 40:6–8) that obedience is preferable to sacrifice (cf. 1 Sam. 15:22).

Thus, the notion that active as well as passive obedience is necessary is not at all counterintuitive to our everyday experience. We often say to someone released from prison, "Your debt has been paid. Show yourself now to be a law-abiding citizen." We recognize that true change manifests itself in a new life of productive work, both in refraining from illegal activities and in pursuing that which contributes positively to the community. Christ's "whole obedience" is a unified way of speaking of the active and passive aspects of His coming to do the Father's will (Heb. 10:7). He does both, and both are imputed to us in our justification so that we have a record of having paid the debt of sin and having kept the whole law.

Some may aver that since Christ paid the debt of sin, it is up to us to provide the righteousness that follows.[5] Indeed, those who trust in the death of Christ alone for

---

If God prefers obedience to sacrifice, it cannot be that Christ's perfect obedience is any less significant than His perfect sacrifice. And it is also unlikely that His obedience was solely to qualify Him to be a sacrifice for us. Rather, both His obedience and His sacrifice were *for us*; consequently, both His obedience and sacrifice are imputed to us (WCF 11; WLC 71). See David VanDrunen, "To Obey Is Better than Sacrifice: A Defense of Active Obedience of Christ the Light of Recent Criticism," in *By Faith Alone: Answering the Challenges to the Doctrine of Justification*, ed. Gary L. W. Johnson and Guy P. Waters (Wheaton, Ill.: Crossway, 2007), 127–46.

5. This was Johannes Piscator's view, set forth herein, as well as that of some recent thinkers. See, e.g., Steve Lehrer and Jeff Volker, "Examining the Imputation of Active Obedience of Christ: A Study in Calvinistic Sacred Cow-ism," accessed at In-Depth Studies Audio, http://idsaudio .org/ids/pdf/classic/imputation.pdf.

their salvation do live grateful lives and serve the Lord, not to pay for sin but because their sin has already been paid for.[6] Yet all such grateful obedience to the law in its third use is far from the perfect obedience that it demands. A holy God can accept nothing less than perfect holiness; the holiness that is a part of our sanctification, being partial and polluted by remaining sin, will never give us a perfect standing before a holy God.[7] We need more than to have our debt paid for by a perfect mediator—we need that same mediator to keep the law for us perfectly. This is what Jesus did in His active obedience, imputing it and His passive obedience to us in our justification.

It was Machen's conviction, then, that the righteousness achieved in Christ's life of perfect obedience while on this earth was imputed to God's people in their justification. That the suffering of Christ to pay the penalty of sin is imputed in justification was a theological

---

6. Sinclair B. Ferguson, *The Whole Christ: Legalism, Antinomianism, and Gospel Assurance—Why the Marrow Controversy Still Matters* (Wheaton, Ill.: Crossway, 2016).

7. This is a point made well by John Calvin (1509–1564) in his *Institutes of the Christian Religion*, ed. John T. McNeill, trans. Ford Lewis Battles, Library of Christian Classics (1559; repr., Philadelphia: Westminster Press, 1960), 3.1–10, who treats regeneration (the new birth and ongoing sanctification) before justification to demonstrate both that the Reformed are not antinomian (as Rome charged) and that all the sanctification conceivable does not yield the perfect righteousness demanded by the law and that it belongs to us only by the imputation of the righteousness of Christ in our justification. We may be as sanctified as possible, yet such an inner work is not sufficient to give us the perfect standing before God that only justification provides.

commonplace in the first generation of Reformers. The conviction that Christ also kept the whole law for His people and that it too was imputed also came to be widely held. Machen simply gave articulate expression to what many hold dear when he admitted that he was grateful for the active obedience of Christ and that he had no hope without it. Clearly, Machen meant to indicate by this admission both that the broken law needed fulfilling and that Christ was the only one who could and did fulfill it. The righteousness He earned in fulfilling it was part of what was imputed to us.

The specific question before us in this book is whether the divines at the Westminster Assembly (1643–1649) affirmed the imputation of Christ's active obedience (hereafter, "active obedience"[8]) for us in our justification. As we shall see, before and during the Assembly a minority of the divines denied active obedience in our justification. In recent years, some among the Reformed have also denied it, arguing that the Assembly did not affirm it clearly. I shall attempt herein to demonstrate that the weight of

---

8. Given the length of the phrase "the imputation of the active obedience of Christ," and its repeated use throughout this work, I will often have recourse to the shortened form "active obedience." It should be noted, however, that usage of such an abbreviated form should not be understood to exclude what is always meant: the active obedience *of Christ*—that is, He kept all the law and did it for His people. The imputation of such active obedience to us is also always in view. Thus, I always mean the "imputation of the active obedience of Christ" even though I use the shortened form "active obedience."

evidence favors the contention that the Westminster Assembly did affirm active obedience.

In so doing, I will briefly survey the question of the affirmation of active obedience before the Reformation, then look at the Reformation (before, during, and after the Westminster Assembly), and finally consider how the church since then has understood the question. We know that theologians in the American Presbyterian tradition, like Machen, Charles Hodge (1797–1878), and others, have affirmed it.[9] So have theologians in the European Reformed tradition, such as Francis Turretin (1623–1687) and Herman Bavinck (1854–1921).[10] But did John Calvin and other early Reformers affirm it, as John Owen (1616–1683) and later Reformers clearly did?[11] I will endeavor herein to answer all of these questions.

---

9. Charles Hodge, *Systematic Theology* (New York: Scribner, Armstrong, and Company, 1871), 3:142.

10. Francis Turretin, *Institutes of Elenctic Theology*, trans. George Musgrave Giger, ed. James T. Dennison Jr. (Phillipsburg, N.J.: P&R Publishing, 1994), 2:445–55, 646–56; Herman Bavinck, *Reformed Dogmatics*, ed. John Bolt, trans. John Vriend, vol. 3, *Sin and Salvation in Christ* (Grand Rapids: Baker Academic, 2006), 377–81.

11. Owen's support for active obedience was manifested in his work on the Savoy Confession (1658), which explicitly affirmed active obedience, especially in 11.1, noting that God justified the elect "by imputing Christ's active obedience to the whole law, and passive obedience in his death for their whole and sole righteousness." Jaroslav Pelikan and Valerie Hotchkiss, eds., *Creeds and Confessions of Faith in the Christian Tradition* (New Haven, Conn.: Yale University Press, 2003), 3:115.

There is, of course, a question behind the issue of active obedience: Why do we need to be justified at all? The answer to this cannot simply be taken for granted, though the treatment that we are able to give it in this work is cursory at best. Let us consider the nature and need for justification more broadly as we endeavor to see where active obedience fits. It is the conviction of the Protestant Reformation that justification is of the utmost importance; in fact, Calvin calls it "the main hinge on which religion turns."[12]

The doctrine of justification is crucial to life. Christians rightly find the crass materialism of our society to be troubling. Is materialism an end in itself, or do those who pursue "stuff" do so ultimately for the acceptance they hope to gain by having such things? Materialism is part of a larger pursuit, not merely of the idols that material possessions may become but of the idol of acceptance. At the deepest levels of our hearts, we want more than simply stuff. We want people to accept us, and one of the ways we sometimes imagine that we will achieve acceptance is by having lots of things: an impressive résumé, beauty, fame, or power.

Acceptance, like comfort, security, control, power, and other felt needs, is one of those things we fully enjoyed before the fall but lost as a result of our sin. Either we come to Christ, and in Him discover the fullness that was lost with paradise, or we make idols of all those things that

---

12. Calvin, *Institutes*, 3.11.1.

we were made to have as part of creation but now lack. Ultimately we should come to Christ and walk with Him because we are called to glorify God, not merely because we want to have our needs met. We are to come to Him while enjoying Him, and part of our enjoyment of God is the wonderful satisfaction we get as we seek to glorify Him in our lives.

Outside of Christ, we do not enjoy God; instead, with restless hearts, we spend the whole of our lives trying to fill up the absence of God with the presence of everything around us.[13] In particular, many make an idol of acceptance and seem willing to do almost anything to gain it. Because the sinful heart suppresses the truth in unrighteousness, it twists and perverts what we really need. We need acceptance, to be sure, but we need it chiefly from God.

For thirsty souls who have found no acceptance and who have come to realize that our lack of a sense of acceptance stems from being sinners who have no acceptance with a holy God, the gospel—that we have acceptance "in the Beloved"—is truly good news. Nothing compares with knowing that we have acceptance—not because of who we are or what we have done but rather despite who we are and what we have done—because of who Jesus is and what He has done. We have an acceptance greater than Adam had in his period of probation because we are fully confirmed by Christ's active and passive obedience

---

13. Augustine, *Confessions* 1.1.1; Pascal, *Pensées*, #425.

and are now as accepted by God as we ever will be (in heaven we will be more happy but not more secure).

The fact that those who are in Christ have acceptance should not simply be taken for granted. When we say we are in Christ, we are speaking of union with Him, which means enjoying by the work of the Holy Spirit all that Christ achieved for us.[14] In His life and death, Christ did all that He did *for us,* and it all becomes ours through union with Him, effectuated by faith. Faith itself is a gift of the Spirit that enables us to "lay hold of" or "believe in" Jesus Christ as He is offered in the gospel. When we exercise faith, the Holy Spirit accounts (or imputes) to us the righteousness Christ achieved by both His active and passive obedience.

This acceptance is a result of our justification, God's great gift to His people. In fact, justification is about how a holy and righteous God can accept sinful men and women. This is a wonderful truth: a pure God, who remains pure, can justly declare wicked men and women, who as a result of sin deserve judgment and condemnation, to be righteous in Christ and thus accepted in the Beloved. Justification is the wonderful reality that, although we remain sinners here below, all those who trust

---

14. A significant bibliography is located at http://philgons.com /resources/bible/bibliographies/union-with-christ/. Of those listed, the more helpful works on union with Christ are those by Todd Billings, John Fesko, Richard Gaffin, Robert Letham, and John Murray; Beeke and Jones are helpful on the period of the Westminster Assembly as they treat the Puritans' views on union with Christ.

in Christ alone have, here and now, perfect acceptance with God, both now and forever. The basis of this acceptance is the active and passive obedience of Christ. Our focus here is how the Westminster Assembly in particular dealt with the question of the imputation of Christ's active obedience in our justification.

1

An Initial Approach to the Westminster Assembly's Understanding of Christ's Active Obedience

In recent years there has been vigorous debate between those who affirm the imputation of the active obedience of Christ in our justification and those who deny it.[1] No

---

1. I heartily affirm active obedience and appreciate the arguments for it adduced by, among others, R. Scott Clark, "Do This and Live: Christ's Active Obedience as the Ground of Justification," in *Covenant, Justification, and Pastoral Ministry: Essays by the Faculty of Westminster Seminary California*, ed. R. Scott Clark (Phillipsburg, N.J.: P&R Publishing, 2007), 229–65; and VanDrunen, "To Obey Is Better than Sacrifice," 127–46. Arguing against active obedience, among others, is Norman Shepherd, "Justification by Works in Reformed Theology," in *Backbone of the Bible: Covenant in Contemporary Perspective*, ed. P. Andrew Sandlin (Nacogdoches, Tex.: Covenant Media Press, 2004), 103–20; Norman Shepherd, "The Imputation of Active Obedience," in *A Faith That Is Never Alone: A Response to Westminster Seminary California*, ed. P. Andrew Sandlin (LaGrange, Calif.: Kerygma Press, 2007), 249–78; Daniel Kirk, "The Sufficiency of the Cross (I): The Crucifixion as Jesus' Act of Obedience," *Scottish Bulletin of Evangelical Theology* 24, no. 1 (Spring 2006): 36–64; and Daniel Kirk, "The Sufficiency of the Cross (II): The Law, the Cross, and Justification," *Scottish Bulletin of Evangelical Theology* 24, no. 2 (Autumn 2006): 133–54. Both Shepherd and Kirk affirm that Jesus was sinless, but only to qualify Him to make atonement, not also *pro nobis* (as our substitute in life as well as death). Both give a tendentious and thin reading of the relevant biblical passages and historical literature.

small part of the debate has been about the role of the Westminster Assembly of Divines and the documents produced by that body.[2] Several sources have historically averred that the Assembly did not affirm active obedience, and more recent sources have repeated that assertion.[3] Others, however, have argued that while the Assembly may never have explicitly affirmed active obedience in what it finally adopted, nonetheless, the Westminster documents, taken as a whole, tend to affirm it.[4] It might be thought that little remains to be added to this discussion.[5]

---

2. The Westminster Assembly of Divines produced a body of documents addressing, among other topics, church government, worship and liturgy, and discipline. The documents that chiefly concern us in this book and that are often called collectively the Westminster Standards (though this sometimes refers to all the products of the Assembly) are the three doctrinal works composed in 1646–1647: the Westminster Confession of Faith (WCF), the Westminster Shorter Catechism (WSC), and the Westminster Larger Catechism (WLC).

3. It is outside the scope of this study to make a full biblical and theological defense of active obedience. My modest aim is simply to seek to demonstrate that the Westminster Assembly did affirm the imputation of the active obedience of Christ and to look at related historical and theological matters.

4. Jeffrey Jue argues this position well in "Active Obedience of Christ and the Theology of the Westminster Standards: A Historical Investigation," in *Justified in Christ: God's Plan for Us in Justification*, ed. K. Scott Oliphint (Fearn, Scotland: Mentor, 2007), 99–130. The assertion that the Westminster Standards tend to affirm active obedience is also made in the Orthodox Presbyterian Church's *Report of the Committee to Study the Doctrine of Justification* (Willow Grove, Pa.: Committee on Christian Education of the Orthodox Presbyterian Church, 2007), 144–45. More recently, this position has been set forth and defended particularly well in John Fesko, *The Theology of the Westminster Standards: Historical Context and Theological Insights* (Wheaton, Ill.: Crossway, 2014), 206–28.

5. Much of the following is drawn from my "The Affirmation of

It is my contention, however, that a few lacunae remain which, when examined, will fill in the picture and permit us to see more clearly that the Assembly affirmed active obedience when it specifically addressed the issue. Although the final language of the Assembly's documents may not have reflected it as some other formulations do (such as the Savoy Declaration of 1658), they reflect a two-covenant structure that affirms (indeed, that entails and requires, especially as seen in chapter 7 of this work) the doctrine of active obedience. Furthermore, I will argue that the original intent of the Westminster divines favors active obedience, as does the interpretation and application of those standards over the years of those churches that have adopted them (in other words, the *animus imponentis* favors such an affirmation). Moreover, the Assembly's constitution as a body to give advice to Parliament rather than as a ruling body of the church materially affected how it did its work; consideration of this is relevant in a variety of controversies, including the question of whether the Assembly affirmed active obedience.[6]

---

the Imputation of the Active Obedience of Christ at the Westminster Assembly of Divines," *The Confessional Presbyterian* 4 (2008): 194–209, 311; and "The Imputation of the Active Obedience of Christ at the Westminster Assembly," in *Drawn into Controversie: Reformed Theological Diversity and Debates within Seventeenth-Century British Puritanism*, ed. Michael A. G. Haykin and Mark Jones (Göttingen: Vandenhoeck & Ruprecht, 2011), 31–51.

6. Two works are particularly helpful in understanding the nature of the Westminster Assembly as a body erected to give doctrinal and ecclesiastical advice to the British Parliament: Robert S. Paul, *The Assembly of the Lord: Politics and Religion in the Westminster Assembly and the "Grand Debate"* (Edinburgh: T&T Clark, 1985); and S. W. Carruthers,

The Claims That the Assembly
Did Not Affirm Active Obedience

The allegation that the Westminster Confession of Faith (WCF) more specifically, or all the Westminster Standards more broadly, does not teach active obedience, or that it at least accommodated those who objected to it, is of some ancient lineage. Mitchell and Struthers treated it in their edition of the Assembly's minutes. They speculated that the alleged omission of explicit language affirming active obedience in WCF 11 was probably to appease prominent Westminster divine Thomas Gataker and others who objected to it. Mitchell and Struthers acknowledged that although most of the divines at the Assembly "favoured the views of [Bishop James] Ussher and [Daniel] Featley," theologians distinctly and vigorously supportive of active obedience (and expressive of such originally), those same divines were later willing to forgo a clear affirmation of active obedience and thus to "abstain from further controversy about the matter."[7]

The Everyday Work of the Westminster Assembly, ed. J. Ligon Duncan III (repr., Greenville, S.C.: Reformed Academic Press, 1994). For a work on the people at the Assembly, see William Barker, *Puritan Profiles: 54 Puritan Personalities Drawn Together by the Westminster Assembly* (Fearn, Scotland: Mentor, 1996). Regarding the ecclesiastical circumstances and theological positions of the divines, see Robert Letham, *Westminster Assembly: Reading Its Theology in Historical Context* (Phillipsburg, N.J.: P&R Publishing, 2009); with respect to justification and the affirmation of active obedience, Letham tends to see the debate as inconclusive, retaining ambiguity (see 250–64).

7. Alex F. Mitchell and John Struthers, *Minutes of the Sessions of the Assembly of Divines* (Edinburgh: William Blackwood and Sons,

The clear implication is that the divines were unwilling to make active obedience a confessional matter and that, in the end, they accommodated those who did not affirm active obedience.[8]

In his history of the Assembly, Mitchell argued more fully along similar lines.[9] Relying chiefly on Daniel Featley's speeches in favor of affirming active obedience, Mitchell correctly noted that on the vote taken on the question of whether Christ's "whole" obedience was imputed to the believer—as a part of the debate on article 11 of the divines' revision of the Thirty-Nine Articles in 1643—"far the major part" of the Assembly voted in favor

---

1874), lxv–lxvii. The reference to avoiding further controversy occurs because Mitchell and Struthers recognize that although early in the Assembly (September 1643) there was controversy over active obedience, there later appeared to be, at the time of the adoption of WCF 11 (in 1645–1646), no further significant debate over active obedience, considerations of which are developed below.

8. James Ussher did not argue for the affirmation of active obedience in the debates at Westminster because, as a devoted Episcopalian, he opposed the meeting of the Assembly (Barker, *Puritan Profiles*, 44–47), and Daniel Featley, although a good source for the 1643 debate on active obedience and a staunch defender of it, was also an Episcopalian, who was arrested just after the justification debates and died in 1645, before the adoption of the Westminster Confession of Faith (Barker, *Puritan Profiles*, 47–50). It is remarkable given the strong animus against Episcopalians how much doctrinal influence Ussher and Featley had. The divines could strongly disagree on matters ecclesiastical but be doctrinally united.

9. Alex F. Mitchell, *The Westminster Assembly: Its History and Standards* (London, 1883; repr., Edmonton, Alberta: Still Water Revival Books, 1992), 149–56.

of affirming active obedience. Why, then, when debating and adopting WCF 11 in 1645–1646, did the divines not adopt the explicit language of whole obedience?[10] Mitchell speculates,

> Probably it was on this account that when the Assembly came to treat of the subject of Justification in their Confession of Faith they left out the word *whole* to which Gataker and his friends had most persistently objected, so that the clause, which in their revised version of Article XI [of the Thirty-Nine Articles] had stood in the form "his *whole* obedience and satisfaction being by God imputed to us" was in the confession changed into "imputing the obedience and satisfaction of Christ," which though it hardly seems to us to include, still less to favour their view, they were content to accept as less rigid than the other.[11]

Mitchell concluded that this was a concession on the Assembly's part that led to "Gataker and his friends" agreeing to "drop further controversy on the question."[12]

More recent historians as well as earlier commentators on the work of the Assembly have argued for some sort of allowance by the divines for a denial of active obedience. William Barker, in his helpful work on the lives of the

---

10. The reason that the date of the debate/adoption of chapter 11 of the WCF will be consistently given throughout this book as 1645–1646 is that, although debate on this chapter took place in 1645, the Assembly did not adopt this chapter until July 1646.

11. Mitchell, *Westminster Assembly*, 155–56.

12. Mitchell, *Westminster Assembly*, 156.

Westminster divines, has characterized this debate over active obedience as one of the areas in which the divines differed among themselves and permitted the difference to remain and not be resolved in favor of a single position. It is his view that the Assembly, as with other questions (like the millennial question and that of the order of the decrees), did not prescribe active obedience and proscribe every other view. Barker argued that, in contrast to Featley (who championed active obedience), William Twisse, Thomas Gataker, and Richard Vines (all of whom Barker contends opposed active obedience) "succeeded in getting the term 'whole obedience' removed from the phrase 'imputing the obedience and satisfaction of Christ unto them' in Chapter XI of the Westminster Confession."[13] Barker concluded that Westminster, when it came to active obedience and some other controversies, "sought to be clear and faithful to Scriptural language, yet to allow for shades of difference within a generic Calvinism."[14] Yet, as we shall see below, no evidence supports the idea that there was any debate whatsoever about having the term *whole* added in 1645–1646 when the Assembly debated chapter 11 of the WCF. That debate was restricted entirely to the discussion held in September 1643 when

---

13. Barker, *Puritan Profiles*, 176.

14. Barker, *Puritan Profiles*, 176. Even in acknowledging that the divines sought to accommodate those who scrupled at active obedience by allowing the omission of *whole* as a modifier of *obedience*, Barker noted that the language of the confession was nonetheless such that the "imputation of Christ's active obedience was thus included," being made explicit in the Savoy Declaration.

the divines were deciding whether to revise article 11 of the Thirty-Nine Articles.

The Counterclaim of This Book

It should be noted that Mitchell, Struthers, Barker, and others who make like observations often do not themselves contest active obedience. Such observers, while personally affirming active obedience, only contend that the Assembly did not ultimately require its affirmation in the standards. Yet others, particularly in more recent times, in arguing that WCF 11 does not require the affirmation of active obedience, have further argued that this is a good thing because they do not believe that active obedience is taught in Scripture. Norman Shepherd, as one who explicitly denies active obedience and who picked up certain strands from Mitchell's history, concluded, "Even the Westminster Confession as late as 1647 was written as a compromise document to accommodate the views of three prominent members of the Assembly (William Twisse [prolocutor of the Assembly], Thomas Gataker, and Richard Vines) who did not subscribe to the imputation of active obedience."[15] But is this a valid conclusion, given several lines of evidence? In this volume I contend that the WCF, taken as a whole, did affirm active obedience and its necessity in the justification of the ungodly. While it is true, as Mitchell, Struthers, and Barker have noted, that the word *whole* as a modifier of obedience is

---

15. Shepherd, "Justification by Works," 115.

not present in the final form of WCF 11 (in 1645–1646), when the debate was fully engaged (in 1643) and involved the men that Shepherd cites (Twisse, Gataker, and Vines), active obedience was clearly affirmed.

The Significance of the Grounds of Justification

I shall pick up this specific debate in chapter 4, but some other matters must be considered before doing that. In the remainder of this chapter, we will look at issues pertaining to the grounds of justification (and the important place of active obedience in that). Additionally, chapters 2 and 3 will furnish important historical background before returning to the debate at the Westminster Assembly.

It might prove useful to pause here, then, even as we have considered in the introduction the nature and necessity of justification, to consider the grounds of our justification, since the active obedience of Christ is centrally involved as the grounds, or basis, of our justification, together with the passive obedience of Christ. Stepping back for a moment, we must recall why we need justification: quite simply, it is because God is righteous and requires all who come into His presence to be righteous. Since the fall we no longer enjoy the righteousness that we did in our state of innocence but have instead become miserable sinners. If we as wicked sinners are to come into God's holy presence, we must somehow come to possess a righteousness that we no longer natively have or can produce. That we who were made holy and who have become sinful are no longer acceptable to the God who remains holy creates an acute sense of lack and need.[16]

This conundrum—how sinful man can purchase or otherwise come to possess the righteousness needed to come into the presence and find the favor of a holy God—sparked the Reformation of Luther, Zwingli, Calvin, and others. As the Reformers put it, How can we sinners find a gracious God, One who will admit us into His favor because He deems us righteous? How God makes the transition from wrath to grace, from being angry with us to forgiving us, and how the sinner thus goes from being rejected to accepted, is, as John Murray termed it, "the basic religious question."[17]

It is not an option for God either simply to declare us righteous contrary to truth (God always acts in accordance with truth) or to forgive sin without requiring its punishment (He never shows love or mercy at the expense of justice).[18] God must somehow declare the

---

16. There are many fine Reformed treatments of justification: John Owen, *The Doctrine of Justification by Faith* (Grand Rapids: Reformation Heritage Books, 2009); James Buchanan, *The Doctrine of Justification: An Outline of Its History in the Church and of Its Exposition from Scripture* (Pelham, Ala.: Solid Grounds Christian Books, 2006); John Fesko, *Justification: Understanding the Classic Reformed Doctrine* (Phillipsburg, N.J.: P&R Publishing, 2008); and K. Scott Oliphint, ed., *Justified in Christ: God's Plan for Us in Justification* (Fearn, Scotland: Christian Focus, 2007).

17. John Murray, *Redemption Accomplished and Applied* (Grand Rapids: Eerdmans, 1955), 117.

18. WLC 71 reflects the reality of the dual maintenance of God's justice, on the one hand, and His love, on the other, with reference to justification. This question addresses the conundrum of how justification

ungodly to be righteous as if they could have both kept the law perfectly and paid the penalty for their transgression of it. But because fallen, unregenerate man is guilty of Adam's first sin as well as all his own actual sin, there is no way that he can either pay his sin debt or render due obedience. If the ungodly are to be justified—that is, declared to be righteous—such a declaration must be based on something extrinsic to them, guilty and polluted as they are by original and actual sin. Thus, it must be on some basis other than what fallen, unregenerate man is or can do that a holy God justifies so as to remain both just and the justifier of the ungodly. The righteousness that we need in order to be justified, but lack because we are depraved, must somehow be furnished by another. It is here that we see the great principle of substitution and imputation.[19] The substitute does for another what that one cannot do for himself, and what the substitute does in

---

is an act of free grace if the grounds of it involves the fulfillment of the demands of God's justice by the obedience and death of Christ. Justification is an act of God's free grace because what God could have demanded of us He accepted from—and provided—a surety, the Lord Jesus Christ, who did for us what we could never do for ourselves.

19. For more than a century, liberal theologians have called the doctrines of substitution "slaughterhouse religion" (Harnack) and imputation "legal fiction." More recently, evangelicals have complained that substitution is "cosmic child abuse." Though restricted to the atonement, Simon Gathercole's *Defending Substitution: An Essay on Atonement in Paul* (Grand Rapids: Baker Academic, 2015) should be consulted; for imputation, see John Piper, *Counted Righteous in Christ: Should We Abandon the Imputation of Christ's Righteousness?* (Wheaton, Ill.: Crossway, 2002).

his living and dying is imputed, or accredited to, the one(s) for whom the substitute acts. With respect to the human race, another who answers to Adam and his progeny must do what Adam failed to do and undo what he did. Our substitute must do for us what we cannot do for ourselves.

Substitution finds its proper and ultimate expression in Christ our mediator, but it was introduced as a principle in the Old Testament. Some would argue that substitution first makes its appearance in Eden, where the Father clothes the first pair with animal skins, replacing their fig-leaf garb. Even more to the point, God institutes the sacrificial system at the time of the giving of the law. In the great revelation of the New Testament, Christ is our substitute both as the "Lamb of God who takes away the sin of the world" and as our surety. As the lamb, our mediator answers to the sacrificial system of the Old Testament. Recall that "the first covenant made with man was a covenant of works, wherein life was promised to Adam; and in him to his posterity, upon condition of perfect and personal obedience" (WCF 7.2). Man, however, "by his fall, made himself uncapable of life by that covenant"; thus "the Lord was pleased to make a second, commonly called the covenant of grace; wherein he freely offereth unto sinners life and salvation by Jesus Christ" (WCF 7.3), the mediator of the covenant of grace.

For the Lord Jesus Christ, the covenant of grace is (as a covenant of redemption with the Father for us) a covenant of works. In other words, in the covenant of grace Christ undertakes to do for us, and to undo, as the second and last Adam, what the first Adam failed to do by violating the covenant of works. This covenant of grace, inaugurated in Eden (Gen. 3:15), is that which is operative after the fall for the elect of God. His people, in the Old Testament as well as the New, are not regarded as "in Adam" but as "in Christ" and thus are made alive (1 Cor. 15:21–22).

The difference, then, between the Old and New Testament economies is not that God's people in the old covenant were saved in a substantially different way than we are in the new covenant. To be sure, we who look back to the person and work of Christ and are made partakers of that accomplished redemption by the Spirit sent in Pentecostal power know a far greater measure of blessing than did our Old Testament forebears who saw salvation only in shadows and types (this being the essential point of the book of Hebrews). But it is the same covenant of grace administered in both Testaments, as noted in WCF 7.5–6:

> 7.5: This covenant was differently administered in the time of the law, and in the time of the gospel: under the law, it was administered by promises, prophecies, sacrifices, circumcision, the paschal lamb, and other types and ordinances delivered to the people of the Jews, all foresignifying Christ to come; which were, for that time, sufficient and efficacious, through the operation of the Spirit, to instruct and build up the elect in faith in the promised Messiah, by whom they had full remission of sins, and eternal salvation; and is called the old testament.

7.6: Under the gospel, when Christ, the substance, was exhibited, the ordinances in which this covenant is dispensed are the preaching of the Word, and the administration of the sacraments of baptism and the Lord's Supper: which, though fewer in number, and administered with more simplicity, and less outward glory, yet, in them, it is held forth in more fullness, evidence and spiritual efficacy, to all nations, both Jews and Gentiles; and is called the new testament. There are not therefore two covenants of grace, differing in substance, but one and the same, under various dispensations.

So we see the basis of our justification: the person and work of our Lord Jesus Christ. This is the gospel, how our Savior fulfilled the just requirements of the law (active obedience) and paid the penalty demanded for its violation (passive obedience). The gospel is the good news to sinners (the law being bad news to man in his fallen state) that, though our sin merits death, Christ, the God-man, has merited eternal life for us by His substitutionary life and death. Given our sinfulness and utter spiritual inability (being, as fallen, "not able not to sin"), we see that our salvation, in its totality, including the grounds for our justification (which is, after all, the justification of the ungodly), must come entirely from outside of us. And it is precisely this need for an external, extrinsic (what Luther and others called "alien") righteousness that the person and work of Christ answers. This is why God became a man—why the second person of the Godhead was incarnated—to provide for us what we sinners need but cannot provide for ourselves. This our Savior does in both His passive and active obedience.

Conclusion

One might also note that the question of whether the Assembly affirmed active obedience is not the only issue contested respecting active obedience. Also disputed is the matter of whether active obedience was affirmed more broadly in the history of the church, particularly preceding the Westminster Assembly. In other words, is active obedience a *novum* that did not make an appearance until the federal theology of the seventeenth century, or did it appear previously in the church and more widely than in just the Reformed and Presbyterian churches? As we have seen, some have implied that active obedience is a *novum*. However, in chapter 2 we shall see that there were some antecedents to active obedience in the ancient and medieval church, and in chapter 3 we will see that there were even more direct progenitors of the doctrine in the Reformation era before the Westminster Assembly.

2

Antecedents to Active Obedience in the Ancient and Medieval Church

As noted in chapter 1, some Reformed writers have claimed that active obedience was a feature present only in the later Reformation. Some of those same writers also dispute that the Westminster Assembly of Divines (in the 1640s) affirmed the doctrine. Such have objected that while the Reformers always affirmed the imputation of Christ's passive obedience in our justification, the earlier Reformers did not affirm active obedience in our justification, and that the later Reformers who did were innovators, at odds with their earlier counterparts. Indeed, some give the impression that the church as a whole, until the later Reformation, only ever affirmed the passive obedience of Christ.

The Works of Christ in the Pre-Reformation Church

In this chapter I contend that the doctrine of Christ's active obedience—His obeying the whole law for us—finds antecedents, albeit in seed form, in both the ancient and medieval church. In fact, one might argue that this aspect of Christ's work (His law-keeping for us) was more clearly treated in earlier times than was the doctrine of the atonement, which was often understood according to the ransom theory, that the death of Jesus on the cross was a ransom paid to the devil.[1] It was only in the Middle Ages, in the writings of Anselm (1033–1109), that the church came to understand that Christ's death was not to pay for something owed to the devil but to satisfy the offended honor (and satisfy the divine justice) of God the Father.[2] This later developed into the propitiatory, substitutionary atonement view treated by Calvin and others.[3]

The Person of Christ before the Reformation

It is worth pausing for just a moment to note that the early church developed the doctrine of the person of Christ far more than the work of Christ. The first seven ecumenical councils, insofar as they dealt with the doctrine of Christ (they also dealt with the doctrines of God and man in particular), tended to focus on His person: the deity of Christ, the humanity of Christ, the relationship of the two natures in one person, whether Christ after the incarnation had only one nature (a divine one), adoptionism, the

---

1. Jaroslav Pelikan, *The Christian Tradition: A History of the Development of Doctrine*, vol. 1, *The Emergence of the Catholic Tradition (100–600)* (Chicago: University of Chicago Press, 1971), 148–51.

2. Anselm, *Why God Became Man*, in *Anselm of Canterbury: The Major Works*, ed. Brian Davies and Gillian Evans, trans. Janet Fairweather (New York: Oxford University Press, 1998), 260–356.

3. Calvin, *Institutes*, 2.16.1–12.

question of Christ's will (did He have one or two?), the iconoclastic controversy, and allied doctrines.[4] As noted above, the precise nature of the atonement was often not extensively dealt with (until Anselm), except for the ransom theory. Interestingly, however, one aspect of the work of Christ was dealt with in the early church (arguably tied to what would later develop in Eastern Christianity as the doctrine of *theosis*): the notion in Irenaeus, Athanasius, and the Cappadocians of Christ recapitulating Adam, succeeding where he failed, assuming humanity so as to redeem it in His infancy, childhood, youth, and manhood.[5]

Active Obedience as Part of Christ's Work Was Understood Early in Church History

The claim of some (like Shepherd and Kirk; see chapter 1) that the early church understood Christ's passive obedience (the substitutionary atonement) and not the active obedience (what we might call the substitutionary life that Christ lived for us) is seen to be false by the testimony of several significant theologians of the ancient church,

---

4. Norman P. Tanner, ed., *Decrees of the Ecumenical Councils*, vol. 1, *Nicaea to Lateran V* (London and Washington, DC: Sheed and Ward / Georgetown University Press, 1990), 1–156.

5. The Cappadocian Fathers (Basil the Great, Gregory of Nyssa, and Gregory of Nazianzus) are often seen as the fountainhead, together with Athanasius, of *theosis*. See Robert Letham, *Through Western Eyes: Eastern Orthodoxy; A Reformed Perspective* (Fearn, Scotland: Mentor, 2007), 243–68. While Protestants take issue with the Eastern Orthodox doctrine of *theosis*, they do not object to, but rather embrace, the teaching that Christ recapitulated Adam.

particularly Justin Martyr, Irenaeus, and Athanasius. Irenaeus's recapitulation theory might be understood as an early version of the doctrine of active obedience.[6] Although Irenaeus's view on recapitulation is often categorized as one of the theories of the atonement, it is arguably more properly a theory involving the life of Christ as much as, if not more than, His death. Perhaps the primary New Testament passage on which Irenaeus based his theory was Ephesians 1:10, which indicates that God's plan for "the fullness of times" is to "gather together in one all things in Christ," the Greek word for "gathering" or "uniting" being rendered in the Latin as "recapitulate."[7] The idea here is that Christ is seen as the new Adam who succeeds where the first Adam failed. The notion that Christ undoes the wrong that Adam did, while containing an atonement conception (Christ died in paying the penalty), chiefly involves Christ obeying where Adam disobeyed, Christ keeping the law that Adam failed to keep, which is the heart of the doctrine of active obedience. Other passages often adduced in support of this are Romans 5:12–21; 1 Corinthians 15:20–21; and 2 Corinthians 5:21.

Irenaeus is considered to be the first to clearly express a recapitulation view of the atonement, although he is anticipated by Justin Martyr, whom Irenaeus quoted in *Against Heresies*: "In his book against Marcion, Justin does well say: '...the only-begotten Son came to us from the

---

6. Pelikan, *Christian Tradition*, 1:144–45.
7. Irenaeus, *Against Heresies* 3.18.7, 3.21.9–10, 3.22.3, 5.21.1.

one God, who both made this world and formed us, and contains and administers all things, *summing up His own handiwork in Himself.*"[8] Irenaeus sets forth his theory of recapitulation in this way: "He [Jesus Christ] commenced afresh the long line of human beings, and furnished us, in a brief, comprehensive manner, with salvation; so that what we had lost in Adam—namely, to be according to the image and likeness of God—that we might recover in Christ Jesus…he [Jesus] became what we are, that He might bring us to be even what He is Himself."[9] I do not deny that there is a focus here on Christ's atoning work, but there is also a focus on the life of Christ in doing what Adam failed to do.

While this is hinted at in Justin Martyr and Irenaeus, it is made more explicit in Athanasius. In his great work *On the Incarnation*, Athanasius, in arguing for the reason and necessity of the incarnation, noted that the eternal second person of the blessed, holy, undivided Trinity "saw the reasonable race of men…wasting out of existence, and death reigning over all in corruption."[10] He saw "that corruption held us all the closer, because it was the penalty for the Transgression; He saw, too, how unthinkable it would be for the law to be repealed before it was

8. Irenaeus, *Against Heresies* 4.6.2 (emphasis added).

9. Irenaeus, *Against Heresies* 3.18.1, quoted in *The Writings of Irenaeus*, ed. A. Roberts and J. Donaldson (Edinburgh: T&T Clark, 1869), 2:55.

10. Athanasius, *On the Incarnation* (Crestwood, N.Y.: St. Vladimir's Orthodox Theological Seminary Press, 1993), 33–34.

fulfilled."[11] Adam, in his first sin and in all subsequent sins, failed to fulfill the law. And if such were never to be fulfilled on behalf of the race, it would be as if the law were repealed without ever having been fulfilled. Athanasius here argued that the reason for the incarnation is not only Christ's passive obedience ("He surrendered his body to death in place of all, and offered it to the Father") but also His active obedience, whereby He fulfilled the law that stood in danger of never being fulfilled because of the sin of Adam and his progeny.[12]

Active Obedience in the Middle Ages

I am unaware of any further substantive discussion contributing to the development of the doctrine of active obedience until the Middle Ages. Heber Carlos de Campos Jr., in his recent dissertation on Piscator, surveys rather extensively the literature for antecedents to the doctrine of active obedience, beginning in the Middle Ages. He finds that Anselm, Abelard, Bernard of Clairvaux, Hugh of St. Victor, Aquinas, and Gabriel Biel all tended to focus on the atonement and passion, although there are expressions (particularly in Bernard, Hugh, Aquinas, and Biel) that might be taken to anticipate active obedience (but this is debatable). He sums up this part of his survey as follows: "Thus, we see that some medieval scholastics did mention the importance of Christ's life

---

11. Athanasius, *On the Incarnation*, 34.

12. Athanasius, *On the Incarnation*, 34–37.

for redemption, though never with a proto-Protestant understanding of Christ's work being imputed. Abelard and Biel highlighted Christ's life more than the others but not with a substitutionary characteristic, but rather with the notion of setting up an example or providing initial merits that need to be complemented with man's response of obedience."[13]

As Campos further notes, "The other aspect that sets up the context for the Reformed discussion of imputed righteousness, especially in [Theodore] Beza, is the scholastic teaching on Christ's redemptive merits from his conception."[14] The implication of this line of thinking is that what Christ merited was for us rather than Himself. Campos notes several medieval thinkers in whom this line of reasoning appears (Hugh, Lombard, Alexander of Hales, Aquinas, Duns Scotus, and Biel). He quotes a work that may have been written by Bernard of Clairvaux: "A triple illness oppresses the human race:...[an] unclean birth, a perverse life, and [a] dangerous death. Christ came, and against this triple disease he brought a threefold remedy. Indeed, he was born, lived, and died: and his

---

13. Heber Carlos de Campos Jr., "Johannes Piscator (1546–1625) and the Consequent Development of the Imputation of Christ's Active Obedience" (PhD diss., Calvin Theological Seminary, 2008), 70. This has been published recently as *Doctrine in Development: Johannes Piscator and Debates over Christ's Active Obedience* (Grand Rapids: Reformation Heritage Books, 2017). This quote is on p. 63 of the published work (quotes hereafter will be from the published work, unless otherwise indicated).

14. Campos, *Doctrine in Development*, 63.

birth purged ours, that death destroyed ours, and his life instructed ours."[15]

Although this might point merely to ethical guidance, "the threefold structure stands out since it is made as a remedial parallel to our triple spiritual disease." Campos concludes his survey of medieval thinkers by noting, "The importance of all this discussion on Christ's merit from conception is that it can be deduced that the Reformed in favor of the [active obedience] were following the [medieval] tradition when they argued that Christ did not need to merit anything for himself throughout his life."[16] In other words, the seed that all that Christ merited was for us, in both His life and death, was planted in the Middle Ages, further contributing to the development of the doctrine of the imputation of Christ's active obedience.[17]

---

15. Campos, *Doctrine in Development*, 64.

16. Campos, *Doctrine in Development*, 65.

17. William D. Lynn, *Christ's Redemptive Merit: The Nature of Its Causality according to St. Thomas* (Rome: Gregorian University Press, 1962), 157. Although Aquinas and others affirmed the merit of Christ, they tended to argue that such is ineffectual unless man adds to the merit of Christ, thus the medieval call to "do one's best" in Gabriel Biel and others, causing problems with and demanding reformation from someone, like a scrupulous Martin Luther. See Heiko A. Oberman, *The Harvest of Medieval Theology: Gabriel Biel and Late Medieval Nominalism* (Grand Rapids: Baker Academic, 2000), 266–70.

The Place of Active Obedience in the Doctrine of the Holy Spirit

We have been looking at developments in the doctrine of Christ, seeking to ascertain the seeds of the doctrine of active obedience. This doctrine, however, is not only, or even chiefly, a concern of Christology but pertains to the doctrine of the Holy Spirit. The debate about active obedience at the Westminster Assembly occurred when the divines were addressing the doctrine of the Holy Spirit, not the doctrine of Christ. This is because the doctrine is not simply about the active obedience of Christ (His lifelong keeping of the moral law) but how that obedience was for us, particularly for our justification. It is important to point this out because this means that in our historical survey we must have in view not only the doctrine of Christ, as we do, but also the doctrine of the Holy Spirit.

The Development of the Doctrine of the Holy Spirit

A bit of reflection on the development of the doctrine of the Holy Spirit more broadly might thus prove useful here. As we have already noticed in this chapter, in the ancient church, particularly in the West, the focus of doctrinal development fell primarily on the early loci in the systematic encyclopedia: the doctrines of God, man, and Christ, especially as developed at the first four ecumenical councils; and the doctrine of the Holy Spirit, particularly the doctrine of the work of the Holy Spirit, received comparatively scant treatment.[18] Even in the extensive development of the doctrine of Christ, however, the doctrine of the *person* of Christ received most of the attention, leaving underdeveloped the doctrine of the *work* of Christ.[19]

As noted earlier, in the Middle Ages the doctrine of the work of Christ received attention particularly in the writings of Anselm, who moved away from a ransom theory of the atonement to one involving the satisfaction of God's offended honor.[20] This progress was not enjoyed by the Eastern church, which remained comparatively underdeveloped in its doctrine of the work of Christ. Since its split in 1054 from the West, the Eastern church

---

18. Tanner, *Nicaea I to Lateran V*, 5–104: The first four ecumenical councils had reference to the Holy Spirit largely to establish His deity. The theology, particularly of the West, in the Middle Ages tended to focus on the matter of the double procession of the Spirit from Father and Son. See Sinclair B. Ferguson, *The Holy Spirit* (Downers Grove, Ill.: InterVarsity Press, 1996), 72–78.

19. Robert Letham, *The Work of Christ* (Downers Grove, Ill.: InterVarsity Press, 1993), 26: "The focus of the first few centuries of the church was on Christ's person, on the eternal relation of Christ to God (the problem of the Trinity) and then on the relation of the divinity of Christ to his humanity (the problem of the incarnation). The work of Christ received little direct attention." A survey of a massive work like Aloys Grillmeier's multivolume *Christ in Christian Tradition*, trans. John Bowden, 2nd ed. (Atlanta: John Knox Press, 1975) amply testifies to this heavy focus on the person of Christ.

20. Anselm develops his doctrine of the atonement in *Cur Deus Homo*, finished in 1098. For a treatment of this in its historical setting, see R. W. Southern, *Saint Anselm: A Portrait in a Landscape* (New York: Cambridge University Press, 1990), 197–227.

has not experienced much development from the time of the seven councils (occurring from the fourth through the eighth centuries), instead emphasizing experience (often mystical) over doctrine.[21]

Although the doctrine of the work of Christ developed in the West in the Middle Ages, the doctrine of soteriology and pneumatology—the application of the accomplished redemption that is ours in Christ, which is to say, the doctrine of the work of the Holy Spirit—lagged. Both the doctrines of the Spirit and of the church were present in Augustine (his mentor Ambrose translated Basil of Caesarea's work on the Holy Spirit; the Eastern church, through the Cappadocians, Athanasius, and others, had developed a doctrine of the Spirit that tended to be mystical). The church in the Middle Ages developed the doctrine of the church, privileging ecclesiology over development of the doctrine of the Spirit. For example, Lombard and Aquinas do not develop pneumatology. Aquinas, in his thirteenth-century *Summa Theologica*, proceeded from the doctrines of God, man, and Christ to the doctrines of the sacraments and the church. A lack of significant development of the doctrine of the Spirit meant that the medieval church, particularly in the High Middle Ages, tended to downplay the divine application

---

21. On this later point of the schism of 1054, as well as the matter of the doctrinal development of the West compared with that of the East, see Jaroslav Pelikan, *The Christian Tradition: A History of the Development of Doctrine*, vol. 2, *The Spirit of Eastern Christendom* (Chicago: University of Chicago Press, 1974), esp. 146–98.

of redemption by the third person of the Holy Trinity and to emphasize the role of the sacraments and of the church, tending, in fact, to fold soteriology and pneumatology into ecclesiology. It is little wonder that, without a vigorous doctrine of the work of the Holy Spirit, the doctrines of the sacraments and of the church overdeveloped and the church embraced the view that the sacraments were efficacious *ex opere operato*.[22]

A More Robust Doctrine of the Holy Spirit's Work

It is not until John Calvin (1509–1564) that we properly develop the doctrine of the work of the Holy Spirit.[23] B. B. Warfield recognized this as the genius of the Protestant Reformation: the merits and mediation of God the Son who accomplished our salvation become ours when the Spirit, by the means of grace, applies them to us.[24] In

---

22. This tendency is seen in the council that serves as the highwater mark of medieval theology—the Fourth Lateran Council (1215). See Tanner, *Nicaea to Lateran V*, 230–71. *Ex opere operato* means "by the working of the work," and the teaching of Rome was that the sacraments conveyed grace to all who received them. Thus, the emphasis was not on the Holy Spirit as the agent who acts to bestow grace through appointed means but on the sacraments themselves, as if they possessed their own power and were efficacious, more or less, automatically.

23. Calvin's *Institutes* comprises a large third book on the Holy Spirit and His work after the second book on Christ and before the fourth book on the church and means of grace.

24. "Here then is probably Calvin's greatest contribution to theological development. In his hands, for the first time in the history of the Church, the doctrine of the Holy Spirit comes to its rights. Into

Calvin's *Institutes*, the doctrine of the Holy Spirit is fully developed after the person and work of Christ are set forth. Calvin recognized that as long as Christ remains outside of us, He does us no good. Calvin followed his discussion of the redemptive work of Christ with a vigorous and full treatment of the Holy Spirit's application of such to God's people.[25] Warfield, in writing on Calvin, understood thoroughly what the Reformation brought to the table that had been missed in the medieval church: we are justified, adopted, sanctified, and glorified, all because of the work of the Holy Spirit to bring Christ to us and us to Christ.

It is little wonder that, although the active obedience of Christ as part of His great redemptive work for us received rudimentary development in the ancient and medieval church, the *imputation* of that active obedience, which is

---

the heart of none more than into his did the vision of the glory of God shine, and no one has been more determined than he not to give the glory of God to another. Who has been more devoted than he to the Saviour, by whose blood he has been bought? But, above everything else, it is the sense of the sovereign working of salvation by the almighty power of the Holy Spirit which characterizes all Calvin's thought of God. And above everything else he deserves, therefore, the great name of *the theologian of the Holy Spirit*." Benjamin B. Warfield, "John Calvin the Theologian," in *Calvin and Augustine*, ed. Samuel G. Craig, foreword by J. Marcellus Kik (Philadelphia: Presbyterian and Reformed, 1971), 487.

25. "First, we must understand that as long as Christ remains outside of us, and we are separated from Him, all that He has suffered and done for the salvation of the human race remains useless and of no value for us." Calvin, *Institutes*, 3.1.1.

distinctly the work of the Holy Spirit, received comparatively little attention until the Reformation. Since it was not until the time of Calvin and afterward that the work of the Holy Spirit received its proper due, it is not to be expected that something like active obedience would even enjoy the proper categories by which to be understood. Since it is the Spirit who takes the merit of Christ and applies it to us (a merit established in His substitutionary passive and active obedience), it is only after the church gained greater clarity about the Holy Spirit's work that it could properly come to understand what followed in the Reformation with the affirmation of active obedience.

3

Active Obedience in the Reformation before the Westminster Assembly

Having surveyed the development of the doctrine in the ancient and medieval church, in this chapter we will examine the question of Christ's active obedience in the time of the Reformation. We will begin by looking briefly at the Lutherans and the Formula of Concord. This will lead us to Calvin, Beza, and others, and it will lead particularly to the Three Forms of Unity. We will briefly survey Piscator's rejection of active obedience and the reaction this elicited. Finally, we will see the place given to active obedience in the most immediate antecedents to the Westminster Standards, particularly the Irish Articles (of 1615).

The Lutheran Treatment

Although Luther spoke of the "great exchange" whereby Christ took our sin on the cross and gave us His righteousness in its place, Melanchthon was the reformational figure who first explicitly taught the doctrine of imputation.[1]

1. Martin Luther, "Instructions to the Perplexed and Doubting, To George Spenlein, April 8, 1516," in *Luther: Letters of Spiritual*

This suggests that Luther and Melanchthon were at least friendly to active obedience, perhaps in seed form. However, neither man explicitly affirmed active obedience, this being left to successors like Martin Chemnitz, who in his *Examination of the Council of Trent* wrote, in view of the inviolable nature of God's law, "For sins this norm requires the fullest satisfaction, and for righteousness it requires the most complete and pure fulfillment of the Law."[2] This is impossible for man in his sinful state, however, and so, Chemnitz wrote, "Since the human race could not make satisfaction to the Law and the Law could in no way be dissolved and destroyed, God made a transfer of the Law to another person (a matter which belongs to the article of justification) who should fulfill the law both by satisfaction and obedience for the whole human race."[3] With Christ as our mediator in His obedience to the law (and in His humanity) in view, Robert Kolb concluded that for Chemnitz, "The human performance [of the divine and human mediator] of fulfilling the demands of the law, in the final analysis, did effect salvation."[4]

Counsel (Vancouver, British Columbia: Regent College Publishing, 2003), 109–38. Cf. Calvin, *Institutes*, 4.17.2. For Melanchthon's views on the doctrine of imputation, see Philipp Melanchthon, *Loci Communes*, trans. Clyde L. Manschreck (Grand Rapids: Baker, 1965), 155–56.

2. Martin Chemnitz, *Examination of the Council of Trent* (repr., St. Louis: Concordia, 1971), part 1, p. 498.

3. Chemnitz, *Examination of the Council of Trent*, part 1, p. 499.

4. Robert Kolb, "Human Performance and the Righteousness of Faith: Martin Chemnitz's Anti-Roman Polemic in Formula of

The matter was decisively, and quite clearly in terms of active obedience, addressed for the Lutherans in 1577 in the Formula of Concord (3.14–15):

3.14: Therefore the righteousness which is imputed to faith or to the believer out of pure grace is the obedience, suffering, and resurrection of Christ, since He has made satisfaction for us to the Law, and paid for [expiated] our sins.

3.15: For since Christ is not man alone, but God and man in one undivided person, He was as little subject to the Law, because He is the Lord of the Law, as He had to suffer and die as far as His person is concerned. For this reason, then, His obedience, not only in suffering and dying, but also in this, that He in our stead was voluntarily made under the Law, and fulfilled it by this obedience, is imputed to us for righteousness, so that, on account of this complete obedience, which He rendered His heavenly Father for us, by doing and suffering, in living and dying, God forgives our sins, regards us as godly and righteous, and eternally saves us.

One may note the presence of the key element involved in affirming active obedience: righteousness is imputed to the believer because Christ has obeyed the law for us. While not being subject to the law Himself, Christ rendered obedience to it "in our stead." While there are

---

Concord III," in *By Faith Alone: Essays on Justification in Honor of Gerhard O. Forde*, ed. Joseph A. Burgess and Marc Kolden (Grand Rapids: Eerdmans, 2004), 132–33.

other soteriological aspects in which we depart from our Lutheran brethren, on this we can agree: it is in living and dying for us that Christ's work is the sole ground of justification.

The Early Calvinist Treatment

No single figure may be more important in this discussion about the Reformed antecedents to an affirmation of active obedience than John Calvin. This is doubtless due to the place of primary importance that Calvin has come to hold: all Reformed and Presbyterian theologians want to have Calvin "on their side" in any given debate if he can honestly be construed as supportive. When it comes to active obedience, where does Calvin stand?[5] The answers usually range from "he did not affirm it" to "he did in substance (though not explicitly) tend to affirm it." I have been persuaded by those who argue in the direction of his implicit affirmation of the doctrine, especially by Cornel Venema's treatment of this. In looking at the relevant issues (the obedience and righteousness of Christ) in Calvin's *Institutes* and in his commentaries and sermons, Venema has conceded that while Calvin did not clearly distinguish the active from the passive obedience of Christ, there is considerable evidence that "Calvin does

---

5. It seems clear to me that Calvin's *Institutes*, 2.16.5 affirms active obedience when he states that "Christ has redeemed us through his obedience, which he practiced throughout his life," as well as elsewhere in the *Institutes*, especially at 2.17, titled "Christ Rightly and Properly Said to Have Merited God's Grace and Salvation for Us."

teach a doctrine of the imputation of Christ's righteousness that includes what later writers distinguished into Christ's active and passive obedience."[6]

Calvin's successor, Theodore Beza, expressed more explicitly the imputation of Christ's positive righteousness in our justification. Heber Carlos de Campos surveys several of Beza's writings, including one in which Beza saw Romans 5:18 as describing a "double righteousness" in which "by the imputed obedience of Christ we are also declared righteous... [since] he fulfilled all righteousness for us" in His keeping of the law on our behalf. Beza expresses such in a variety of places, particularly in one of his theological letters, speaking of Christ becoming a man without sin so that He would "both fulfill the law and pay the penalties of our sin, so that integrity, justice and satisfaction for us are... in him imputed by the inserted faith." Campos, in speaking of this epistle, notes that it "argues that the whole earthly life of Christ from conception to ascension should be considered as one absolute obedience for us, an obedience with an active and a passive side to it."[7]

Some recent writers have asserted that Zacharias Ursinus denied active obedience. Campos, however, does not believe that Ursinus's *Commentary on the Heidelberg Catechism* is consistent and clear on the matter, although it does contain evidence suggesting that Ursinus questioned

---

6. Cornelis Venema, "Calvin's Doctrine of the Imputation of Christ's Righteousness: Another Example of 'Calvin against the Calvinists'?," *Mid-America Journal of Theology* 20 (2009): 46.

7. Campos, *Doctrine in Development*, 85.

active obedience. This is not insignificant, since Ursinus, together with Caspar Olevianus, is taken to be a chief composer of the Heidelberg Catechism. At the end of the day, Campos finds the evidence for both Ursinus and Olevianus to be inconclusive,[8] which is quite interesting in light of Heidelberg Catechism 60–61, which clearly seem to affirm active obedience:

Q. 60: How are you righteous before God?

A. 60: Only by true faith in Jesus Christ. Even though my conscience accuses me of having grievously sinned against all God's commandments, of never having kept any of them, and of still being inclined toward all evil, nevertheless, without any merit of my own, out of sheer grace, God grants and credits to me the perfect satisfaction, righteousness, and holiness of Christ, as if I had never sinned nor been a sinner, and as if I had been as perfectly obedient as Christ was obedient for me. All I need to do is accept this gift with a believing heart.

Q. 61: Why do you say that through faith alone you are righteous?

A. 61: Not because I please God by the worthiness of my faith. It is because only Christ's satisfaction, righteousness, and holiness make me righteous before God, and because I can accept this righteousness and make it mine in no other way than through faith.

---

8. Campos, *Doctrine in Development*, 88–106.

One may note several things from these two questions that favor the doctrine of active obedience. The sinner is said to lack all merit, which highlights for us that the drafters believed that merit is necessary to come into the presence of a holy God. This merit that we lack comes as an act of "sheer grace," in that God grants and credits something to the sinner. In other words, in justification, God imputes, accounts, or attributes something to the sinner that he needs but lacks and that is utterly alien to him. What God grants is the "perfect satisfaction, righteousness and holiness of Christ," which is to say that He grants the merit of Christ. For the justified one, then, it is as if "I had never sinned nor been a sinner, and as if I had been as perfectly obedient as Christ was obedient for me." All of this is so, as HC 61 says, "because only Christ's satisfaction, righteousness, and holiness make me righteous before God."

If there is any question as to whether the Three Forms of Unity clearly affirm that the merit of Christ is what constitutes our righteousness before a holy God, article 22 of the Belgic Confession makes this clear: "But Jesus Christ is our righteousness in making available to us all his merits and all the holy works he has done for us and in our place." In all that Christ accomplished, He did it not for Himself (that being unnecessary) but "for us and in our place." And because all His holy works and merits are made available to us (accessed through faith), Christ is our righteousness, doing for us what Adam failed to do and what we are incapable of doing: keeping the law in our stead (as well as dying for us, who have broken the law in Adam and in our own lives).

The Minority Report of Piscator Opposed

As noted throughout this work, Johannes Piscator became the first, particularly in response to the affirmation of active obedience by Beza, to argue that the imputation of Christ's righteousness was restricted to His obedience in making satisfaction for the sins of His people. A minority of Reformed theologians joined him in this. But in the aftermath of Piscator's denial, many Reformed theologians rose to oppose him and to affirm active obedience. Some of this opposition, of course, found its way into the Reformed confessions.

One of the Reformed confessions that served particularly as an antecedent to the Westminster Confession of Faith was the Irish Articles of 1615, drafted largely by James T. Ussher, the archbishop of Armagh, who was also appointed to and consulted by (though never in attendance at) the Westminster Assembly of Divines. Here are the sections in the Irish Articles relevant to the matter of active obedience:

> 30. Christ in the truth of our nature was made like unto us in all things, sin only excepted, from which he was clearly void, both in his life and in his nature. He came as a Lamb without spot to take away the sins of the world by the sacrifice of himself once made, and sin (as Saint John saith) was not in him. He fulfilled the law for us perfectly: For our sakes he endured most grievous torments immediately in his

soul, and most painful sufferings in his body. He was crucified, and died to reconcile his Father unto us, and to be a sacrifice not only for original guilt, but also for all our actual transgressions. He was buried and descended into hell, and the third day rose from the dead, and took again his body, with flesh, bones, and all things appertaining to the perfection of man's nature: wherewith he ascended into Heaven, and there sitteth at the right hand of his Father, until he return to judge all men at the last day.

34. We are accounted righteous before God, only for the merit of our Lord and Saviour Jesus Christ, applied by faith; and not for our own works or merits. And this righteousness, which we so receive of God's mercy and Christ's merits, embraced by faith, is taken, accepted, and allowed of God for our perfect and full justification.

35. Although this justification be free unto us, yet it cometh not so freely unto us that there is no ransom paid therefore at all. God showed his great mercy in delivering us from our former captivity, without requiring of any ransom to be paid, or amends to be made on our parts; which thing by us had been impossible to be done. And whereas all the world was not able of themselves to pay any part towards their ransom, it pleased our heavenly Father of his infinite mercy without any desert of ours, to provide for us the most precious merits of his own Son, whereby our ransom might be fully paid, the law fulfilled, and his justice fully satisfied. So that Christ is now the righteousness of all them that truly believe

in him. He for them paid their ransom by his death. He for them fulfilled the law in his life. That now in him, and by him every true Christian man may be called a fulfiller of the law: forasmuch as that which our infirmity was not able to effect, Christ's justice hath performed. And thus the justice and mercy of God do embrace each other: the grace of God not shutting out the justice of God in the matter of our justification; but only shutting out the justice of man (that is to say, the justice of our own works) from being any cause of deserving our justification.

It is quite evident that Ussher affirms active obedience in these sections of the Irish Articles. This is what Piscator opposed, emboldening some others to join him in opposition to active obedience but encouraging many more, in the vein of Ussher, heartily to affirm active obedience.

The Nature of Justifying Faith

The active and passive obedience of Christ, as we have seen, furnish God with a basis, or grounds, for justifying us. We have seen that the justification of the ungodly, which speaks to our situation after the fall, is made possible because Christ's righteousness is imputed to us even as our sin was imputed to Him—Luther's "glorious exchange." In fact, Luther came to recognize that the righteousness that we as sinners cannot produce but that a holy God unalterably requires is given freely to us as a gift. And the gift of righteousness that God gives, imputing to us the merits and atonement of Christ, is received by faith alone.

Justifying faith is said to be alone but not because it is ever alone "in the person justified." Indeed, true saving faith "is ever accompanied with all other saving graces, and is no dead faith, but worketh by love" (WCF 11.2). This means that faith, while indeed a gracious work of the Spirit of Christ in the hearts of the elect, whereby they are enabled to believe to the saving of their souls, is also that by which a Christian believes to be true "whatsoever is revealed in the Word." Such faith acts in accordance with what each particular Bible passage contains: "yielding obedience to the commands, trembling at the threatenings, and embracing the promises of God for this life, and that which is to come" (WCF 14.2).

So saving faith, broadly conceived, may rightly be said to be living and active. Such faith always produces obedience and results in faithfulness. Even so, saving faith, while active, expresses itself in its principal acts not by its acting (or its fruits—faithfulness, obedience, good works) but by its "accepting, receiving, and resting upon Christ alone" (WCF 14.2). The primary action of faith, then, if it may be put this way, is not that faith "does something" but that faith "stands there," looking entirely away from self—from all that one has, is, and does—to rest in another, who does everything for the one thus resting and trusting. Such "accepting, receiving, and resting upon Christ alone" is not only for justification but also for sanctification and eternal life as a whole (WCF 14.2). This assertion of our confession as to the receptive/resting character of faith highlights the reality that salvation is all of grace in all its parts and that the heart of faith involves a looking away from ourselves entirely to rest and trust in Christ alone.

Justifying faith, as something that may be distinguished from sanctifying faith, for instance, both as a part of saving faith, is explicitly defined in WLC 72:

Q. What is justifying faith?

A. Justifying faith is a saving grace, wrought in the heart of a sinner by the Spirit and Word of God, whereby he, being convinced of his sin and misery, and of the disability in himself and all other creatures to recover him out of his lost condition, not only assenteth to the truth of the promise of the gospel, but receiveth and resteth upon Christ and his righteousness, therein held forth, for pardon of sin, and for the accepting and accounting of his person righteous in the sight of God for salvation.

Note that as regards man, justifying faith involves an utter despairing of any ability to save oneself; as it regards God, it involves a receiving and resting on Christ and His righteousness as the sole basis on which a person is accepted and accounted as righteous in the sight of God for salvation.

Question 72 of the Larger Catechism also highlights that this receiving and resting "upon Christ and his righteousness" is something more than merely assenting to "the truth of the promise of the gospel." To be sure, justifying faith is never *less* than assenting to the truth of the gospel. Indeed, the church has rightly taught that faith involves (1) knowledge, (2) assent, and (3) trust. Faith has at least a minimal intellectual content—one must know the basic facts of the gospel—in contrast to Rome's assertion of implicit faith (that you need not understand; that the church will understand for you and you should believe what the church tells you to believe) or liberalism's reduction of faith to feelings (emphasizing the trust aspect at the expense of knowledge, as Friedrich Schleiermacher did in speaking of Christianity as merely a "feeling of absolute dependence"). Knowledge is not enough, however, as one may know a great deal of the Bible and not believe it. Neither is belief, or assent, enough. The demons believe and tremble (James 2:19). Question 72 reminds us that knowledge and assent need to be completed by trust and that justifying faith always involves not only assent to the truth but a trust expressed in receiving and resting on Christ. As a believer receives and rests on Christ and His righteousness, he receives pardon of sin and is accounted as righteous before God.

Having seen how faith is never alone in the person justified but accompanied by all other saving graces, we need to see precisely how it is that faith justifies a sinner in the sight of God. This is the question posed by WLC 73:

Q. How doth faith justify a sinner in the sight of God?

A. Faith justifies a sinner in the sight of God, not because of those other graces which do always accompany it, or of good works that are the fruits of it, nor as if the grace of faith, or any act thereof, were imputed to him for his justification; but only as it is an instrument by which he receiveth and applieth Christ and his righteousness.

This question and answer points out that, although faith is not alone in the person justified, it is faith alone that is instrumental in justification.

The aloneness of faith highlights that, as it pertains to justification, faith is a receiving and resting that is to be distinguished from everything else properly associated with, accompanying, and flowing from justifying faith. As WLC 73 affirms, faith justifies a sinner, but not because of the other graces that accompany it. Repentance, for instance, is clearly a grace—a gift—that always accompanies justifying faith (WCF 15.1, 3). Repentance, however, is not in view in our justification. While the initial act of justifying faith is accompanied by sorrow for and hatred of sin (repentance), repentance plays no role as such in our justification, in which faith is solely instrumental.

Furthermore, WLC 73 teaches that the faith that justifies does not do so because of the good works that are the fruit of it. True faith always has good works as its fruits. Such good works, however, while indicating our justification, are no proper part of the declaration of justification itself as a forensic act. Good works are even distinguished from the other graces (like repentance) that accompany faith; they are said to be fruits of faith, not that which accompanies faith, and thus are further distinguished, but not separated, from justifying faith itself.

Finally, WLC 73 seeks to make it clear that justifying faith does not do so "as if the grace of faith, or any act thereof, were imputed to him for his justification." In other words, it is not our exercise of faith that becomes our righteousness, as if faith itself were the righteousness that God requires and the exercise of which would earn such righteousness for us. No, faith is but an instrument, the open hand, that God must give us, by which alone we "receiveth and applieth Christ and his righteousness."

The point of all this is that justifying faith is something that has reference to its object rather than itself. Christ in the totality of His person and work is our Savior, and faith involves a "looking to Him alone" quality (what is often called extraspective, a looking outside of oneself). Faith, because its efficacy rests in its object, need not be robust to be saving. While we should seek to strengthen our faith by all the appointed means, even weak faith, as long as it is true faith in Christ, is saving. This is why our Lord said that faith but the size of the smallest seed (Luke 17:6) is enough, because saving faith characteristically looks away from itself to its object, and since the object is Christ, all true faith, weak though it may be, is saving.

The Opposition of Piscator and Others

This reality runs counter to the tendency of some proponents of the New Perspective on Paul or of the Federal Vision to merge faithfulness (which is the fruit and effect of faith) into faith itself and always to present true faith as something that is extraordinarily robust. In such a schema, in which faith is required to be full if it is to be saving, Christ can tend to be eclipsed, an overstuffed notion of faith leading to an emaciated view of the person and work of Christ, in which all that Christ has done for us (in His active and passive obedience) need not apply to us, but only the atoning work of Christ. A biblical conception of faith is thinner, faith itself not including within it all its accompaniments and fruits, and thus Christ, faith's object, is of necessity more robust. Magnify faith, and one diminishes Christ. Recognize that even the best of us have a rather weak faith, comparatively, and Christ in the fullness of His person and work *pro nobis* (for us) will that much the more be eagerly sought.

Piscator's opposition to active obedience was in response to the evolution of active obedience as the Reformation continued to develop. Piscator was not wrong to observe that a nascent federal theology was developing, arguably present in Calvin in seed form,[9] which would continue to develop and blossom in the work of many Reformed theologians, even finding expression in Reformed and Presbyterian confessions such as the Irish Articles and the Westminster Standards.[10] According to Campos,

---

9. Peter Lillback has effectively argued that, although Calvin did not explicitly affirm the covenant of works and other aspects of federal theology, such were present in seed form in his theology. *The Binding of God: Calvin's Role in the Development of Covenant Theology* (Grand Rapids: Baker Academic, 2001).

10. See chapter 7 of this work for a treatment of federal theology. After Westminster, active obedience found explicit expression not only in the Savoy Declaration but in countless Reformed theologians. See also Campos, *Development of Doctrine*, 226–40.

Piscator understood that justification consisted in its entirety of the remission of sins imputed to the believer. Justification, then, was a *simplex actio Dei*, the imputation of a one-part righteousness. He found basis for this understanding in the several passages of Scripture which tied justification to the blood or the cross. For him, Scripture never indicated Christ's life of obedience to the law being imputed to the believer. Moreover, he believed that the imputation of Christ's active obedience raised contradictions within theology: if Christ's life makes one righteous then there is no need for the cross; if Christ's obedience makes us right with the law, then God's punishment upon Christ to satisfy the law is an unjust requirement of a double payment; if Christ obeyed in our behalf then we are freed from the obligation to obey God's moral law.[11]

Theologians were not the only ones to deliver a significant response to Piscator and the minority who held to his position. The church more broadly, in its confessional expression, also did so. The most direct ecclesiastical response was at the French Reformed synods of Privas (1612) and Tonneins (1614).[12] Privas contained fourteen articles, all of which focused on the relationship of Jesus Christ to the law, arguing that His keeping of the law

---

11. Campos, "Johannes Piscator," vii.

12. These French Reformed synods, especially Tonneins, were very much the concern of the English King James I in his commitment to ecumenism. For James's involvement in Tonniens and Dort, see W. B. Patterson, *King James VI and I and the Reunion of Christendom* (New York: Cambridge University Press, 1997), 155–95, 260–92.

was not something that He was bound to do as a human but was done entirely vicariously and as our substitute — that is, as the mediator between God and man.[13] These were international synods, as was the one held at Dort (1618–1619), at which Arminianism was condemned.

James I, in his various instructions to the British delegates at Dort, indicated that he wanted the synod meeting there to steer clear of theological niceties (whether this might include active obedience is not clear), particularly as he wanted as much harmony as could be achieved among Reformed European Christendom.[14] While Dort did not ultimately address this issue, just before this, in James's own dominion, Ussher had taken a rather strong stand in the Irish Articles on the work of Christ, both in His active and passive obedience and its imputation to us in our justification. All this is to say that between French synods refuting Piscator and the Irish Articles, there was clear confessional precedent to the affirmation of active obedience (even if such appears to be missing from the Synod of Dort[15]), setting the stage for the Westminster Assembly of Divines.

---

13. Campos, *Development of Doctrine*, 181–83.

14. Anthony Milton, ed., *The British Delegation and the Synod of Dort*, Church of England Record Society 13 (Woodbridge, Suffolk: Boydell Press, 2005), esp. 92–94.

15. Milton, *British Delegation*, xlviii: It is clear that the British delegation at Dort opposed Piscator for the same teachings that even the Remonstrants did, although not necessarily for his position on the denial of active obedience.

4

The Work of the Westminster Assembly and Active Obedience, Part 1

Having surveyed briefly the ancient, medieval, and earlier Reformation-era antecedents to or affirmations of active obedience (as well as denials by Piscator and company), we now return to examining the fate of the doctrine at the Westminster Assembly. The affirmation of active obedience at the Assembly in 1643 has only recently come to fuller light. While Mitchell and others knew of this debate, we did not have all the minutes (or Lightfoot's journal) from that debate until now, thanks to the seminal work done by Chad Van Dixhoorn as part of his doctoral dissertation at Cambridge University.[1] Historians now must look to this work for the fuller picture of the

---

1. Chad Van Dixhoorn, "Reforming the Reformation: Theological Debate at the Westminster Assembly, 1643–1652" (PhD diss., University of Cambridge, 2004). This is a seven-volume work, with the first volume containing Van Dixhoorn's thesis proper and volumes 2–7 consisting of appendices containing, among other things, Lightfoot's *Journal* and the *Minutes of the Westminster Assembly* from September 4, 1643, to March 25, 1652. This is now the most complete printed representation of these records. More recently, Van Dixhoorn edited (with

great justification debate that took place at the Assembly in 1643. We see in these materials, to which even a contemporary historian like Barker did not have access, that when the Assembly fully debated the matter of active obedience, it did so in a way that clearly affirmed this doctrine. Jeffrey Jue has recently done a good job recounting this history, based on the more recent work of Van Dixhoorn, and has also concluded that, on the whole, the Assembly affirmed active obedience.[2] Jue's work should be consulted, along with Van Dixhoorn's, for the fuller argument. A few points, however, that fill in and complement the work of Jue and Van Dixhoorn might be helpful here.

The Original Work of the Westminster Assembly on Justification

When the Assembly came into session on July 1, 1643, it did not begin drafting a confession of faith (or a form or government or directory for worship, for that matter). Rather, in its initial attempts to reform the Church of England further (the Church of Scotland would

---

David F. Wright) *The Minutes and Papers of the Westminster Assembly, 1643–1653*, vols. 1–5 (New York: Oxford University Press, 2012).

2. Jue, "Active Obedience of Christ," 121–28. See esp. p. 126, where Jue addresses the fact that the word *whole* does not appear as a modifier to *obedience* in the final version of what the Assembly adopted. Jue concludes, as I do in this book, that although the historical record throws no clear light on the precise reason for *whole* not being finally employed to modify *obedience*, the overall "two-Adam Christology" of the Westminster Standards clearly militates against the denial of active obedience.

come later), Parliament tasked the Assembly with revising the already existing articles of faith that the English church had employed since the time of their drafting in the reign of Edward VI (1547–1553) and their restoration in Elizabeth's reign (1558–1603): the Thirty-Nine Articles of the Church of England. The Assembly began working methodically through the Thirty-Nine Articles shortly after coming into session in July 1643, and the divines reached the article on justification, article 11, in September 1643.[3]

In the Thirty-Nine Articles, only article 11 treats justification. This is significant because there are so many aspects that the Reformation addressed regarding the doctrine of justification: its nature and necessity (both of the godly and of the ungodly), its grounds, the nature of justifying faith, double (and triple) imputation, and so on. Article 11, as the only place addressing justification in the Thirty-Nine Articles, had to bear the entire weight of all the major aspects of the doctrine of justification. It was thus in the interest of the Assembly, insofar as its original task doctrinally was restricted to revision of the Thirty-Nine Articles, to be as precise (and concise) as possible in the revision of article 11 so as to give maximal Reformed

---

3. In addition to the background materials on the 1643 revisions to the Thirty-Nine Articles furnished by Mitchell and Struthers in *The Minutes of the Westminster Assembly* (see lxv and elsewhere for article 11 on justification), see R. M. Norris, "The Thirty-Nine Articles at the Westminster Assembly" (PhD diss., University of St. Andrews, 1977), lv–lviii. Van Dixhoorn gives extensive treatment to this in "Reforming the Reformation," 1:270ff.

expression to the doctrine of justification in the comparatively minimal space of one article. The WCF, however, enjoyed considerably greater space to develop the doctrine of justification; a whole chapter (with five subsections) was devoted to it and was also spread throughout other WCF chapters and over a number of Shorter and Larger Catechism questions.[4] This original restriction of having to express everything about justification in article 11 meant that the Assembly was pressed to say all that it wanted to about justification in a relatively brief space and that precision was at a premium.

The original article 11 as earlier adopted by the Anglican Church and before any amendment of the Assembly in 1643 was as follows: "We are accompted righteous before God, only for the merit of our Lord and Saviour Jesus Christ by faith, and not for our own works or deservings. Wherefore that we are justified by faith only is a most

---

4. Jue points out that an affirmation of active obedience is integral to other places in the Westminster Standards, like WCF 7 (on covenant) and WCF 8 (on Christ the mediator), as well as WLC 70, 92–93, in addition to WCF 11, which is directly on justification. WCF 8.5 speaks of the "perfect obedience and sacrifice of himself," and WLC 70 affirms the "perfect obedience and full satisfaction of Christ." The conjunction *and* in both cases suggests that this "perfect obedience" is in addition to the "sacrifice" and "full satisfaction" of Christ and that both are, as WLC 70 affirms, "by God imputed to them." This affirms that not only the death of Christ (the sacrifice that fully satisfies Adam's and the elect's violations of the law) but also His life is substitutionary (*pro nobis*) because both the perfect obedience and the full satisfaction of Christ are imputed to us for our justification. Jue, "Active Obedience of Christ," 126–28.

wholesome doctrine, and very full of comfort; as more largely is expressed in the Homily of Justification." After other amendments had been made to this article, the proposed revision that occasioned the debate about adding the word *whole* to modify *obedience* was as follows: "We are justified, that is, we are accounted righteous before God, and have remission of sins, not for nor by our own works or deservings, but freely by his grace, only for our Lord and Saviour Jesus Christ's sake, his whole obedience and satisfaction being by God imputed unto us[;] and Christ with his righteousness, being apprehended and rested on by faith only, is an wholesome Doctrine, and very full of comfort: notwithstanding God doth not forgive them that are impenitent, and go on still in their trespasses."[5]

The Debate over "Whole Obedience"

As noted, other revisions were made to article 11 than the addition of the word *whole* as a modifier of *obedience*. However, all students of this debate agree that nothing occasioned greater contention than this modification; all also agree that the addition of the word *whole* was a short-handed way of affirming active obedience.[6] Arguably, there

---

5. Both the original and revised texts are given in Van Dixhoorn's "Reforming the Reformation," 1:270, 320, respectively.

6. Van Dixhoorn, "Reforming the Reformation," 1:271. Lightfoot regarded this 1643 justification debate as "our great question," engendering a "hot debate." See Lightfoot, MS Journal, folios 32v, 30v, 35r, 35v, 26r. Richard Baxter, now widely regarded as a neonomian, was quite interested in the Assembly's debate and had correspondence with several members about his own doctrine of justification, which, like

may have been better ways of affirming active obedience than this particular wording. As Van Dixhoorn notes, "Some divines, even some advocates of the imputation of the active obedience of Christ, felt the language of whole obedience was itself ambiguous. [Active obedience champion] Daniel Featley initially urged that the Assembly use the language of the imputation of the 'perfect satisfaction and righteousnesse of Christ.'"[7]

It is perhaps worth noting, particularly in support of Jue's contentions, that language outside of the specific chapter on justification that would later be adopted at the Assembly (the wording of WCF 8.5 and 11.1–3, for instance) is in these very terms: WCF 11.3 speaks even more fully about a "proper, real, and full satisfaction to his Father's justice in their behalf" and distinguishes between Christ's "obedience and satisfaction," with the word *both* signifying that such obedience and satisfaction are "accepted in their stead" (implying that Christ is our substitute in death *and* life so that both the active and passive obedience is imputed to us). It is hard to see how this is any less than Featley, as one of the stalwart defenders of active obedience, would have wanted.[8] This observation supports the contention that even the WCF in its final form, both

this debate, came to be seen as a "hot peppercorn." For a discussion of which, see the fine study by H. Boersma, *A Hot Pepper Corn: Richard Baxter's Doctrine of Justification* (Zoetermeer: Boekencentrum, 1993).

7. Van Dixhoorn, "Reforming the Reformation," 1:328.

8. Much of this paragraph derives from the OPC's *Report of the Committee*, 144n289, to which this writer was a primary contributor.

in chapter 11 and elsewhere, affirmed active obedience, regardless of whether the word *whole* modified the word *obedience* at any place in the Westminster Standards.[9]

In considering the debate over the word *whole* at the Assembly and the affirmation of active obedience, it is important to note that the main theological error among Protestants, at least as far as the Assembly was concerned, and which it determined to oppose, was antinomianism.[10] To be sure, Romanism concerned the divines, especially with regard to the doctrine of justification, and the Assembly sought to refute Rome's errors carefully at every point. The same is true of Arminianism, although there is some dispute as to whether the divines took a clear position on Amyraldianism.[11] A number of factors point to

---

9. Fuller consideration of this claim is found in chapter 6 of this work.

10. Van Dixhoorn, "Reforming the Reformation," 1:276ff. A number of more recent works have highlighted the "threat" of antinomianism in Britain at the time of the Assembly. See, e.g., David R. Como, *Blown by the Spirit: Puritanism and the Emergence of an Antinomian Underground in Pre-Civil-War England* (Stanford, Calif.: Stanford University Press, 2004), 64ff.; David Parnham, "The Covenantal Quietism of Tobias Crisp," *Church History* 75, no. 3 (September 2006): 511–43; and David Parnham, "Motions of Law and Grace: The Puritan in the Antinomian," *Westminster Theological Journal* 70 (2008): 73–104. Quite helpful in understanding the challenge that antinomianism posed at the Westminster Assembly itself, particularly with regard to the debate on "whole obedience" and the broader concern over the affirmation of active obedience, is Whitney G. Gamble's *Christ and the Law: Antinomianism at the Westminster Assembly* (Grand Rapids: Reformation Heritage Books, 2018), esp. 87–108.

11. Mitchell and Struthers (*Minutes*, 152) would indicate that

the chief doctrinal concern being antinomianism, perhaps because it was an error often wrongly associated with the Assembly's view that salvation was entirely by grace alone. In view of earlier confessions having condemned Roman and Arminian error, the Assembly wanted to make it clear that the gracious character of the salvation that it confessed was in no way at odds with the requirement that Christians pursue holiness and live a godly life.[12]

Thus, the Assembly condemned the foundational antinomian error of eternal justification, out of which various antinomians of the time developed doctrines claiming that Christians are not bound by the third use of the law and that God sees no sin in His children, so they need not pray "forgive us our sins."[13] The antinomians of

---

Westminster divine Edmund Calamy was an Amyraldian. Warfield and others would also note Richard Vines, Lazarus Seaman, and Stephen Marshall among that number, although Warfield argued that the expressions made in WCF 3.6, 8.5, and 8.8 would militate against any hypothetical universalist position. See Benjamin B. Warfield, *The Westminster Assembly and Its Work* (New York: Oxford University Press, 1931), 56.

12. Gamble, *Christ and the Law*, 39–64.

13. Van Dixhoorn, "Reforming the Reformation," 1:307: "Francis Taylor openly sided…with Gataker, Vines, and Woodcock…by raising the antinomian issue. As Taylor saw it, if 'Christ hath performed the law for me, then it will follow I an [am?] not bound to keepe this lawe myself.'" Then, Van Dixhoorn makes a most telling observation: "Fear of catering to antinomianism was far more real to most divines than the likelihood that they would stumble into one of the heretical pitfalls" associated with antinomianism. In view of this, it is significant that the divines gave such a vigorous affirmation of the free grace of God manifested in justification.

this period tended to collapse everything into either the eternal decrees or the work of Christ (we could say *pactum salutis* and *historia salutis*), giving short shrift to the necessity for the Christian to walk in and strive for holiness (tending to see the Christian as passive in all parts of the *ordo salutis*). The Assembly was deeply troubled by this corruption of the gospel and, in fact, at the time of the great debate on justification (fall 1643), also had a committee of some of its members consulting with Parliament as to how certain antinomian publications should be handled and antinomianism suppressed.[14]

Given, then, that antinomianism posed the kind of threat that it did, at least as far as many of the Westminster divines perceived it, it is little wonder that the Assembly took great care to give that error no quarter. In fact, the determination to yield no ground to the antinomian or to do nothing to give aid and comfort to antinomianism played no little part in the debate over the affirmation of active obedience.[15] In the course of the 1643 debate, it became plain that, among the few divines who opposed the affirmation of active obedience, all of them opposed antinomianism, and many of them took the position that they opposed active obedience because of their opposition to antinomianism. The divines were

---

14. Carruthers, *Everyday Work of the Westminster Assembly*, 125ff.; Paul, *Assembly of the Lord*, 176–82. See the Humble Petition of the Assembly to Parliament concerning antinomianism in Lightfoot's journal (Van Dixhoorn, "Reforming the Reformation," 2:26–28).

15. Gamble, *Christ and the Law*, 65–84.

quite aware that certain antinomians were only too glad to hear and would likely misconstrue any affirmation of active obedience. This makes all the more noteworthy the Assembly's overwhelming affirmation of active obedience. Although the Westminster divines knew that antinomians might misuse the affirmation of active obedience, because they believed such to be at the heart of the gospel, they affirmed it anyway as a testimony to the free gospel of Christ.[16] Just as the Assembly did not let fear of antinomianism keep it from affirming active obedience, neither should we let any such fears keep us from likewise testifying to the truth.[17]

The debate on article 11 involved not only the addition of the word *whole* as a modifier of *obedience* but also a number of amendments before and after the debate on *whole*, including debate over what to title the article.[18] All observers agree, however, that the real debate was over the addition of *whole*, and thus over the question of active obedience. Richard Vines, an opponent of the affirmation

---

16. Lightfoot had great disdain for the antinomians and made it clear that the Assembly's contempt for such played no little role in the debate, even prompting a few to oppose active obedience on the grounds that such opposition would militate against antinomianism (see, for example, Van Dixhoorn, "Reforming the Reformation," 2:31). Lightfoot, though a strong opponent of antinomianism, was a strong proponent of the affirmation of active obedience.

17. Historical antinomianism is a perennial problem. See Ferguson, *Whole Christ*; and Mark Jones, *Antinomianism: Reformed Theology's Unwelcome Guest* (Phillipsburg, N.J.: P&R Publishing, 2013).

18. Van Dixhoorn, *Minutes*, 3:12.

of active obedience, spoke first in the debate and argued that since justification means "the remission of sins," he assigns such strictly "to the passive obedience of Christ." He argues that the passive sufferings of Christ are the proper matter imputed.[19]

Throughout this debate, the few opponents of active obedience typically would argue along these lines, observing that Christ's active obedience was that which He was due to yield as a part of His humanity in the incarnation and that such was necessary to make Him fit to be our sin bearer in the passive obedience, in His death on the cross. Thus begins the debate, with rejoinders to Vines coming from divines who raise issues about whether Christ as the second person of the Holy Trinity was bound to keep the law for Himself (as opposed to keeping it for us), claiming also that references to Christ's obedience are synecdochal and that one cannot separate His active and passive obedience.[20]

Thomas Gataker, who became the chief opponent of the affirmation of active obedience in the Assembly's debates, also responded.[21] He argued somewhat differently from Vines, however, contending that justification itself is merely legal and does not have in view the

---

19. Van Dixhoorn, *Minutes*, 3:25.

20. Van Dixhoorn, *Minutes*, 3:25.

21. An excellent volume sheds further light on Gataker and the handful of others who agreed with him (in opposition to the majority "orthodox" opinion): David Parnham, *Heretics Within: Anthony Wotten, John Goodwin, and the Orthodox Divines* (Brighton, UK: Sussex Academic Press, 2014), esp. pp. 33–36.

remission of sins. Since Gataker tended to separate the remission of sins from the forensic declaration and saw justification as applying only to the latter, he also tended to refer the grounds of justification to the work of Christ, separating that from the definition of justification, narrowly construed.[22]

William Twisse, the prolocutor of the Westminster Assembly, who is often said to have opposed the affirmation of active obedience (though there is never any clear opposition expressed in the minutes),[23] came at the question of justification from yet another perspective. He believed in eternal justification, as did the antinomians, although there is no evidence that he shared in the errors that the antinomians drew from their affirmation of eternal justification. Twisse did, however, warn the

22. See Lightfoot's journal in Van Dixhoorn, "Reforming the Reformation," 2:48ff., for the shape of the great justification debate.

23. Barker, *Puritan Profiles*, 176, claims that Twisse joined Gataker and Vines in opposing active obedience. But this contention is not substantiated. Twisse, as a supralapsarian, was particularly concerned with any teaching that savored of synergism like Roman Catholicism and Arminianism (see Barker, *Puritan Profiles*, 29). Twisse's writings bear out his supralapsarian convictions. See *Treatise concerning Predestination* (London: J. D. for Andrew Crook, 1646); and *The Riches of Gods Love unto the Vessells of Mercy, Consistent with His Absolute Hatred or Reprobation of the Vessells of Wrath…* (Oxford: Printers to the University, 1653). This last work contains a particularly vigorous defense of the supralapsarian order in the decrees. If for some reason Twisse did oppose active obedience in justification, it was not because he believed salvation to be anything than utterly monergistic. His alleged opposition would not threaten the utter graciousness of justification.

Assembly about too strenuously opposing the antinomians.[24] One thing is clear: if he opposed active obedience, which remains unclear and contested, he did not do so on the grounds that it would lend aid and comfort to the antinomians, given that he himself was concerned about Assembly overreaction to antinomianism. It may be that he referred the doctrine of active obedience to sanctification and not justification. At any rate, Twisse, being the supralapsarian that he was, would have been no friend of anyone wanting to introduce any element of human merit or works (as a part of our faithfulness) into the equation of our justification.[25] To put this in terms of contemporary debates, for Federal Vision (FV) partisans or their allies to cite Twisse in support of denying active obedience is like citing Herman Hoeksema in support of FV monocovenantalism, even though Hoeksema's monocovenantalism is of a different stripe altogether.[26]

---

24. Van Dixhoorn, *Minutes*, 3:19. His reason(s) for doing so is (are) not perfectly clear, although one might surmise, from other things that he wrote, that he was concerned lest the Assembly fall into the opposite error and also because he did believe in eternal justification (which the Assembly came ultimately to deny; WCF 11.4).

25. Chad Van Dixhoorn, "The Strange Silence of Prolocutor Twisse: Predestination and Politics in the Westminster Assembly's Debate over Justification," *The Sixteenth Century Journal* 40 (2009): 395–418.

26. OPC, *Report of the Committee*, 117.

The Nature of Deliberative Assembly Debate

It ought to be remembered that lengthy debate does not necessarily signify a good deal of disagreement among the debaters. Heated debate, like the 1643 debate over the addition of the word *whole*, often indicates that some participants feel very strongly about the issue at hand, not that the body debating is highly divided.[27] Those of us who have served in many church judicatories, especially General Assemblies of our respective denominations, can testify that it takes only a few parties with strong views on an issue to engender significant and heated debate. But when it comes time for the vote, even after lengthy debate, it is sometimes revealed that the body is not highly divided over the issue and that the temperature of the debate stemmed from a handful of men with strong views; when those few have exhausted their speeches, the final vote is not close.[28] In the great justification debate of 1643, Gataker spoke twenty-five times and

---

27. See Van Dixhoorn, *Minutes*, 3:32, in which something of the Assembly's debate psychology can be gathered from the remarks of an active obedience defender (Walker), who makes the following point to those vigorously debating against active obedience: "[We, advocates of active obedience] desire [that] they [opponents of active obedience] would not think we yield the cause because [we do] not answer things answered before." In other words, because the few opponents of active obedience were vigorously combating it and making many speeches against it does not mean that the "silent majority" did not remain strongly supportive of active obedience.

28. Such a situation occurred at the 2007 GA of the PCA; following what appeared to be significant debate, the body voted, by more than 90 percent (according to several witnesses), to affirm the report of

Vines twenty-three times: these two were among the top four speakers in the debate.[29] In other words, those who opposed the affirmation of active obedience spoke a lot during the debate, yet when it came to the vote, only three or four men out of fifty voted against affirming active obedience.[30] This means that the vote in favor of affirming active obedience was in excess of 90 percent, even if there were four voting against it.

Only those inexperienced in church deliberative bodies would wonder how such a vigorous debate might yield such a lopsided vote. Those more familiar with the ways of such bodies know that such is not uncommon. Novitiates may express surprise that vigorous debates can lead to one-sided conclusions, not realizing that most people do not speak in a debate and that the most fervent speeches are often given by a small minority strongly opposed to the motion under consideration and committed to the employment of every reasonable debate tactic to secure its defeat. Gataker, Vines, and a few others ultimately exhausted their say and were unconvincing to their fellows. When the vote came in session 52 at the close of the Tuesday morning session on September 12, 1643, only three or four are said to have dissented, and even at that none had their negative votes recorded save Gataker,

---

a committee that had found certain teachings of the New Perspectives on Paul (NPP) and FV to be confessionally deficient.

29. Van Dixhoorn, "Reforming the Reformation," 1:332.

30. Van Dixhoorn, *Minutes*, 3:77.

initially at least; for some reason he thereafter changed his mind and asked that his negative vote be stricken.[31]

This 1643 debate over the addition of the word *whole* to modify *obedience* is the only record of such a debate over active obedience.[32] The other citations in the Assembly minutes, which include every reference at the Westminster Assembly to the doctrine of justification, read as follows: "2 Dec. 1645; 23 July 1646; and 4 Feb. 1647 (Minutes 3:113r, 281v or 166v, 303v or 195v). For the debates on the text of the chapters, see 3, 8–11, 16 Dec 1645; for the Scriptures see, 10, 11 Feb. 1647 (Minutes 3:113r–115r, 123v–124r)."[33] There is no record for any of these dates, when checked in the minutes concerning the confession of faith and catechisms, of any debate on justification, not to mention active obedience, comparable to that held in September 1643 when the Assembly voted to affirm active obedience by retaining the language of "whole obedience."

Insofar as it is alleged that the dissent in this debate points to a lack of agreement on active obedience, it is the case that none of the divines availed themselves of the protocol that Parliament had established whereby members might express dissent.[34] Lest it be thought that such

31. Van Dixhoorn, *Minutes*, 3:77; in note 7 on this page the record shows, "'dissenting. Mr. Gataker,' 'Mr. Gataker' erased."

32. What follows in this paragraph comes from the OPC's *Report of the Committee*, 143n287.

33. Van Dixhoorn, "Reforming the Reformation," 1:324nn234–35.

34. See Lightfoot's journal in Van Dixhoorn, "Reforming the Reformation," 2:3–4: On July 6, 1643, both houses of Parliament sent to

a mechanism was never employed, in the same general time frame as the 1643 justification debate, Cornelius Burgess objected to a particular action of the Assembly and invoked the established avenues of dissent.[35] Gataker did nothing of the sort when it came to the vote over-whelmingly affirming active obedience. Although Gataker seems to have originally asked to have his dissenting vote recorded, he had his name as a dissenter stricken from the record. Even this mildest of dissents, recording one's negative vote, was abandoned by Gataker, and none of the stronger forms of dissent available were ever engaged. Gataker did nothing further than what even the most vigorous dissenters (and Gataker was undoubtedly that) seemed willing to live with when it became clear that active obedience had been affirmed.

It is regularly asserted that the Westminster Standards involve compromise, making it possible for all parties to

---

the Assembly a set of eight "general rules" of procedure. Rule 7 set forth that "no man [is] to be denied to enter his dissent from the Assembly, and his reasons for it at any point," and if subsequent debate in the Assembly does not yield satisfaction, the dissenting party may have it sent to Parliament not as the concern of a particular man but as a point not capable of clear resolution by the Assembly. Rule 8 makes further provisions for dissent. Recourse to such rules was never taken by Gataker or others who may have opposed the Assembly's affirmation of active obedience in 1643.

35. See Lightfoot's journal in Van Dixhoorn, "Reforming the Reformation," 2:40ff. Here Lightfoot began to report on what he regarded as great contentiousness on the part of Burgess in opposing certain features of the Solemn League and Covenant, invoking the previously mentioned rules of dissent.

live comfortably with the finished product.[36] On certain issues, such compromise is clear, particularly in cases in which the Assembly chose to prescribe less than what a majority of its members might otherwise affirm on an issue.[37] But when the Assembly debated the question of active obedience, it was clearly affirmed, even in the face of strong, albeit few, dissenters. Although the Assembly afterward did not choose this precise language, it should not be assumed that it changed its mind on the issue or that it sought to provide a berth wide enough to make all its members, both the many who did and the few who did not affirm active obedience, comfortable.

---

36. Sinclair B. Ferguson, "Westminster Assembly," in *The Dictionary of Scottish Church History and Theology* (Downers Grove, Ill.: InterVarsity Press, 1993), 863–64. Ferguson, referring to the debate about Amyraldianism, states, "In some matters, we find indications that the Divines were concerned to express a generic Reformed theology in such a way that a certain latitude of interpretation would be possible." While the original intent of the Assembly appears to have been not to proscribe Amyraldianism, it appears to affirm active obedience.

37. J. V. Fesko, "The Westminster Confession and Lapsarianism: Calvin and the Divines," in *The Westminster Confession into the 21st Century*, ed. L. Duncan (Fearn, Scotland: Mentor, 2004), 2:477–525. Fesko treats here an area about which the divines exercised genuine theological latitude: the Assembly dealt with the lapsarian question so as to affirm infralapsarianism without decidedly ruling out supralapsarianism. Warfield put it a bit differently: "The Supralapsarians… and the Infralapsarians… set down in the Confession only what was a common ground to both, leaving the whole region which was in dispute between them entirely untouched." *Westminster Assembly and Its Work*, 56.

In regard to the contention that the Assembly, though clearly affirming active obedience in 1643, backed off of it in 1645–1646 as a necessary compromise to accommodate Gataker and others, it should be noted that the nature of the Assembly, as a consultative body, never required such compromise. Members were never asked to subscribe to all the revisions to the Thirty-Nine Articles or, later, to all the chapters of the WCF, as if the Assembly were a church court with power to compel compliance and, failing such, to excommunicate. In other words, no vote taken at the Assembly, on any particular issue, meant that all were in agreement with what had been adopted as if they all subscribed to it. Here is the point: active obedience was affirmed in the revision of article 11 in 1643, and there is no reason to suppose that it was not also affirmed in WCF 11 and in the other relevant chapters of the WCF, even though the specific wording of revised article 11 never again appears. It is my contention that it did not need to appear in that form because the wording of WCF 11.3 and 8.5 did everything that the revision of article 11 by the addition of the word *whole* was intended to do (and arguably more).[38]

The Later Treatment of Justification at the Assembly

One might speculate that something like theological exhaustion set in between the first debate on justification

---

38. Chapter 6 of this work treats this contention more fully.

(1643) and the treatment given justification in the WCF (1645–1646). This putative exhaustion could mean that when it came time to adopt the confessional statement about justification in 1645–1646, the divines had little heart to engage again in the kind of intense theological debate that they had in 1643. Perhaps in order to avoid the kind of fight that the Assembly underwent in 1643, and particularly to accommodate opponents to active obedience like Gataker and Vines, one might suppose that the Assembly decided to forgo the matter and not make an issue of "whole obedience." Two considerations, however, need to be taken into account before entertaining the possibility of theological exhaustion. First of all, as noted above, in 1643 the entire freight of the argument for active obedience rested on the word *whole*. But in 1645–1646 the Assembly no longer had simply one article to work with in terms of justification and active obedience but rather an entire chapter and more.

Second, the role of those who objected to active obedience in 1643, although never rising to the level of formal dissent in the immediate aftermath of the affirmation of active obedience, is somewhat unclear in the years that followed. Scholars seem to assume that Gataker, Vines, Twisse, and perhaps others must have agitated for the removal of the word *whole*—that is, for the effective repeal of the 1643 affirmation of active obedience—and must, in some measure, have been successful since "active" obedience is not clearly delineated in the subsequent confession or catechisms. What role did Gataker, Vines, and

Twisse play after the 1643 debate? The record simply does not say, but there are some clues that Twisse and Gataker, specifically, may have played a very small role. As noted above, whatever his role was in the justification debate,[39] Twisse, having been ill and missing many sessions, died between session 676 (July 17, 1646) and 677 (July 22, 1646). In session 678 on July 23, 1646, the "report was made by Mr. Arrowsmith 'of Justification and Adoption.' The Report was debated, and upon debate agreed to; and it is as followeth [in our current WCF, chapters 11–12]."[40] Thus, Twisse was not present at the adoption of WCF 11. Furthermore, it is unclear what role Gataker played, if any, in the 1645–1646 debate; his health "after the first two years of the Assembly…forced him to curtail his activities."[41]

The Reasons for the Later Silence on "Whole Obedience"

Speculation abounds as to why, as some see it, the Assembly affirmed active obedience in 1643 but left it ambiguous in 1645–1646.[42] It is Mitchell's opinion that, although "far the major part [of the Westminster Assembly] voted for the affirmative, that Christ's whole

---

39. The rest of this paragraph is from the OPC's *Report of the Committee*, 141n284.

40. Mitchell and Struthers, *Minutes*, 258–59.

41. Barker, *Puritan Profiles*, 159.

42. The rest of this paragraph is from the OPC's *Report of the Committee*, 143n288.

obedience was imputed to the believer," Daniel Featley, a major advocate for affirming the whole obedience, yielded to the dissenters because the question of active obedience was new and not disputed in previous centuries. "Probably," Mitchell continued, "it was on this account [of several factors, including the newer nature of the question] that when the Assembly came to the treatment of the subject of Justification in their Confession of Faith [in chapter 11] they left out the word *whole* to which Gataker and his friends had most persistently objected." The dissenters were content to accept chapter 11 as less rigid than the earlier revised article 11. Mitchell cited Simeon Ashe's funeral sermon for Gataker as maintaining that "Gataker and his friends agreed to drop further controversy, the matter having been conceded."[43]

Van Dixhoorn tends also to read the evidence, on balance, as indicating that the Assembly ultimately adopted a consensual position (that would accommodate those scrupling at affirming active obedience),[44] although he

---

43. Mitchell, *Westminster Assembly*, 155–56.

44. Van Dixhoorn, "Reforming the Reformation," 1:324–30, esp. 326. Van Dixhoorn notes that in drafting its catechisms, the Assembly may have considered adding something explicit about active obedience. Because the Assembly did not explicitly affirm it as the Savoy Declaration later did, Van Dixhoorn concludes that the Assembly's decision "not to use the language of active obedience of Christ" was "deliberate," and thus it "appears that the Assembly chose not to make its statement as clear as possible." Further, it is possible in the two to three years between the two main debates over justification "a critical number of divines may have changed their minds over the necessity of the doctrine in a national confession" (328). I think that to make

cites possibly counterevidence as well, such as how Ashe's funeral sermon for Gataker is to be interpreted: "Other comment on the conclusion of the debate is provided by Simeon Ashe, where he cites Gataker's silence at the end of the debate as an example of his peace-loving spirit. Ashe also brings up Gataker's "resolutions" not to publish his discourses on Romans 3:28, "that he might not publikely discover his dissent from the Votes of that Reverend Assembly."[45] The clear implication is that the Assembly codified a doctrine of justification with which Gataker could not agree. Unfortunately, Ashe and Gataker do not say if he is referring to Gataker's silent opposition to votes on the eleventh article (which would tell us nothing new) or votes on the eleventh chapter of the confession, which would suggest that Gataker understood the Assembly's final text, even with its increased ambiguity, to be teaching a view opposite his own. Gataker's own comment on the matter is also ambiguous: he states that Twisse and "one of the Independent partie" agreed with his views, but the majority of the Assembly did not.[46]

---

for as much peace as possible, the divines chose not to reintroduce the word *whole* because they used other words to express the same thing. I appreciate Van Dixhoorn's pacific approach here but point out that he himself admits that there is no clear evidence that the divines changed their minds over the necessity of the doctrine in a national confession. The only supposed evidence is that *whole* no longer modifies *obedience* at any point.

45. Van Dixhoorn, "Reforming the Reformation," 1:329.

46. This paragraph is also from the OPC's *Report of the Committee*, 143–44n288.

The debate in which active obedience was hotly disputed occurred in September 1643, before the English Parliament had concluded the Solemn League and Covenant (SLC) with the Scots in October 1643. The SLC changed the entire character of the Assembly and the documents that it would produce.[47] The Assembly had already been established by an act of Parliament and had begun meeting on July 1, 1643. Thus the Assembly, as originally constituted, was not for the reforming of the church in the two kingdoms of England and Scotland (as it was *after* the SLC) but for the reform of the Church of England, particularly the revising of the Thirty-Nine Articles. It was while working for the reform of the English Church, then, that this great battle over active obedience in justification occurred.

---

47. For much of this history, see W. D. J. McKay, "Scotland and the Westminster Assembly," in Duncan, *Westminster Confession into the 21st Century*, 1:213–45.

5

The Work of the Westminster Assembly and Active Obedience, Part 2

Given that the original task of the Westminster Assembly was not to propose a new confession of faith but to revise the already existing Thirty-Nine Articles of Religion, along with suggesting revisions for the government, discipline, and worship of the church, it might prove helpful to reflect on the circumstances surrounding Parliament's calling of the Assembly.[1] The majority in Parliament, the House of Commons more specifically, after the calling of the Long Parliament of 1640, was clearly Puritan in its sympathies. As such, the Commons tended to oppose both the high church innovations referred to as Laudianism, more particularly, and episcopacy, more broadly, with many in the Commons preferring some form of established presbyterianism or congregationalism. The Assembly was largely of this mind as well.

---

1. As noted above, Carruthers and Paul are helpful for this, as is Van Dixhoorn, "Reforming the Reformation," 1:12–54, on the "calling and constitution of the Westminster Assembly," all of which were consulted especially for the following paragraphs.

The Assembly diverged from Parliament, however, on the question of the relationship between the church and the state. While there were a few Erastians in the Assembly, who tended to view the church as under the state and its creation, the Assembly, urged on by the Scots after they came, generally opposed Erastianism.[2] While many in the Assembly would quickly and eloquently counsel that the church should be able to maintain a province distinct from, and in no way inferior to, that of the state's, few in the Commons would agree, as they wanted to retain Erastian control over the church. Thus, while Laudianism tended to be opposed by all in Parliament and in the Assembly, the same could not be said for Erastianism, with few in the Assembly supporting it whereas many in Parliament did. While all students of this history know that Parliament called the Westminster Assembly into session, the implications of Parliamentary Erastianism—particularly its effect on the relative power that the Assembly thus enjoyed, or failed to enjoy, as a result of a dominating Parliament—seem often overlooked.

When it comes to questions of what the Assembly intended doctrinally to proscribe and to prescribe, too little is made of the reality that this body was called to meet by the state, not the church (it was not a synod and had none of the powers of the General Assembly). Provoked by certain Laudian and divine-right episcopal

---

2. Hugh M. Cartwright, "Westminster and Establishment: A Scottish Perspective," in Duncan, *Westminster Confession into the 21st Century*, 2:181–221.

claims, Parliament, in reaction to this and to the "Root and Branch Petition" in late 1640, moved to abolish the episcopacy and to call an assembly of divines that could serve to advise Parliament as to further reform of the church. Accordingly, Parliament established and named an assembly that was its own, "and no other['s]," creature.[3] This assembly was not a convocation, as ordinarily conceived, "or in any sense 'a court of the church.'"[4] In terms of the perennial question of church over state (as Rome taught) or state over church (as Caesaropapism had it in the Middle Ages and Erastianism in the Reformation), England had largely, at least in the monarchy and her governing bodies, embraced the state over church model since the time of the Reformation under Henry VIII (ca. 1531). This Erastian model prevailed even at the time of the Westminster Assembly and rendered that body purely advisory to Parliament, impacting something of the way that it did its work and of how we should view the products of that Assembly.

The Way the Assembly Worked

Perhaps a bit of historical perspective would be helpful in comparing the Westminster Assembly to other bodies that addressed matters of Christian doctrine. It is the case that after the conversion of Constantine (312), civil authorities regularly convened ecclesiastical assemblies.

---

3. Carruthers, *Everyday Work of the Westminster Assembly*, 21.
4. Carruthers, *Everyday Work of the Westminster Assembly*, 21.

But the nature of such convocations was usually for the purpose of addressing particular errors or condemning certain heresies, unlike Westminster, which was called to address the further reformation of the Church of England broadly. Constantine himself, for instance, called the Council of Nicaea (325) to secure the purity, peace, and unity of the church with regard to the Arian controversy. That council ended with all those present (except for two) signing off on the condemnation of Arianism (with the two dissenters also being condemned). Councils in the ancient and medieval church, whether called by civil rulers or not, typically on their own authority and together with papal approval as that became more prominent, condemned various views and defined the faith in authoritative ways. The Westminster Assembly, however, was not a body that had the authority of itself to condemn views and then compel those who held such condemned views either to recant or to suffer excommunication.

In other words, the Westminster Assembly did not have the same power as General Assemblies or even lower judicatories of the church. As far as Reformed synods were concerned, following the ecumenical councils of the earlier church, the Synod at Dort (1618–1619) was the Reformed body to which Westminster looked in the execution of its work. Dort was an assembly called by the state to deal with the crisis in the Dutch Reformed churches precipitated by the Remonstrants (followers of Arminius), who challenged Reformed orthodoxy. Dort condemned Arminianism, dismissing the Remonstrants from its meetings and giving the state warrant to deal with the Arminians as those whom the church, acting in solemn synodical council, had determined to censure. Westminster had no such power of church censure, much less to order the state to reprimand those whose teachings it might have proscribed.

No one was on trial at Westminster, nor could that body enact church discipline solely on its own authority. While the civil magistrate in Scotland did promulgate the various documents produced by the Westminster Assembly, such never happened in England. This was due especially to the triumph of Oliver Cromwell, including the execution of Charles I, which led to the defeat of all those who opposed Cromwell and the regicide (most of the Presbyterians in England and Scotland, with many Presbyterian parliamentarians removed by Pride's Purge). In other words, all the advice given by the Westminster Assembly to English Parliament was never officially taken (although it was among the Scots).

It is not necessary to assume that if Westminster decided something in a certain way, this must have meant that it was a compromise position to accommodate divines who held different positions on a given issue. We know that members of the Assembly held different positions on certain issues and that, in some of these cases, the Assembly adopted a compromise position to accommodate the varying views. We need not assume, however, that simply because Westminster decided a controverted issue in a certain way that such a decision necessarily entailed compromise. Indeed, the Assembly might choose a briefer rather than fuller affirmation to accommodate a minority that would object to the fuller statement. A minority of brethren favored independency, but this does not mean that the Westminster Assembly accommodated that position. Because the Assembly chose not to prescribe certain positions does not mean that it chose to prescribe no positions. We know that the Assembly clearly affirmed active obedience when it held a distinct vote on the question in 1643. There is no evidence whatsoever that the Assembly ever repealed that affirmation. And the absence of another debate about justification in 1645–1646 does not count as evidence in favor of the Assembly backing off on the affirmation of active obedience.

Did the Westminster Assembly Accommodate on Active Obedience?

In regard to the contention that the Westminster Confession of Faith reflects an accommodation to those who denied active obedience, or what is often referred to as a consensual expression in WCF 11 (comprising both the supporters and deniers of active obedience), Van Dixhoorn has noted that "perhaps the strongest evidence of favour of reading the Assembly's *Confession* in a consensual fashion, is the fact that when the Independents revised and then reissued the Assembly's *Confession of faith* in 1658, they inserted the language of the 'active and passive obedience' of Christ into their version of the

Confession."[5] The addition made to the Savoy Declaration in its chapter 11 is arguably stronger than what was adopted by the Westminster Assembly. That this addition represents a significant one to Westminster needs to be demonstrated from primary sources. It is noteworthy that Philip Schaff did not regard Savoy's addition to WCF 11 as one worth mentioning in the changes that Savoy made to the WCF.[6] One might argue, then, that what Savoy did to modify chapter 11 in its revision of the WCF was not regarded as something clearly different from Westminster but that it served only to clarify and make explicit the WCF's specific point on active obedience.

As noted above, Norman Shepherd distinctly appeals to the lack of explicit affirmation of active obedience in the WCF as an accommodation to the views of Gataker, Vines, and Twisse. We have seen that such a claim is speculative at best. At worst, it is suspect, with Shepherd seeking to shore up his position by appealing to something for which we have no clear evidence. It may be worth noting, in the larger scheme of things, that even if the documents produced by the Westminster Assembly could be shown to support Shepherd—that is, the lack of the word *whole* in WCF 11, in contradistinction to

---

5. Van Dixhoorn, "Reforming the Reformation," 1:330. For the full text of the 1658 Savoy Declaration, see Jaroslav Pelikan, ed., *Creeds and Confessions of Faith in the Christian Tradition* (New Haven, Conn.: Yale University Press, 2003), 3:104–35.

6. Philip Schaff, ed., *The Creeds of Christendom* (repr., Grand Rapids: Baker, 1985), 3:718. This paragraph derives from the OPC's *Report of the Committee*, 144n290.

its adoption as part of the revision of article 11 in 1643, means that the Westminster Assembly did not require the affirmation of active obedience—such a position would not necessarily amount to what Shepherd and others contend. Wes White has shown that even in the case of those for whom we have evidence as deniers of active obedience—Ursinus (who may have denied active obedience after 1566) and Piscator (who inarguably denied active obedience)—Shepherd's citation of those denials is to little effect since he differs from all of these men in his broader theological construction. As a prime example, Shepherd's view of the nature of justifying faith is not the same as Piscator's or Westminster's.[7] On that score alone, even if Westminster did not explicitly affirm active obedience, its theology as a whole tracks quite differently from Shepherd and others, and it cannot be appealed to for any support of them.[8]

---

7. J. Wesley White, "The Denial of the Imputation of the Active Obedience of Christ: Piscator on Justification," *Confessional Presbyterian* 3 (2007): 147–54. This article demonstrates conclusively that Shepherd's redefining of faith as faithfulness means that works has been imported into it and thus his system is not even the same as other deniers of active obedience, like Piscator, who retained traditional Reformed definitions of faith alone. See also White's key article in this regard, "Saying 'Justification by Faith Alone' Isn't Enough," *Mid-America Journal of Theology* 17 (2006): 256–66.

8. Unlike Norman Shepherd, prime active obedience opponent Thomas Gataker argued that while "faith justifies a man, works justify faith" (*fides justificat hominem, opera justificant fidem*), clearly distinguishing faith from that which demonstrates it and shows it to be true. That Gataker and Vines take different approaches from Shepherd

In fact, Shepherd denies the two-covenant approach, which holds that Christ did for us in the covenant of grace what Adam failed to do in the covenant of works. Shepherd's denial of Christ's keeping the law for us—which supporters of active obedience contend He did not simply for Himself in order to qualify as our spotless sacrifice—together with his denial of the two-covenant framework (to which active obedience is foundational) means that Shepherd's system of doctrine is different from the one contained in the Westminster Standards. Shepherd, not unlike some others in the history of the Reformed church, has both affirmed the Westminster Confession (and claimed its support in its alleged refusal to affirm active obedience) and, at the same time, called for its revision, particularly in terms of it teaching what he calls a works-merit paradigm.[9] But if the Westminster Standards present us with such a paradigm, one would not think them worthy of affirmation (even as we view Tridentine doctrine) but foundationally flawed. Since these standards, together with the other Reformed standards,

---

and FV allies in their treatment of justification can be seen in all the recorded remarks that they make in debate in Van Dixhoorn, "Reforming the Reformation," 2:46–87, 3:11–77; and Thomas Gataker, *An Antidote against Errour, concerning Justification* (London: Henry Brome, 1670).

9. Both in his article, "Justification by Works in Reformed Theology," esp. 115–17, and in his online critique of the OPC's *Report of the Committee*, Shepherd has argued against the idea of the covenant of works (as confessed in WCF 7), regarding it as part of the "works-merit paradigm" and thus calling for revision of the WCF.

shape and define what is properly called the Reformed faith, to disagree with them at such a fundamental level is not to think them in need of minor revision but to think them unworthy of subscription. Whatever such a departure from the standards entails, it certainly means that those departing are not Reformed, whatever it is that they may be.

6

The Imputation of Christ's Active Obedience throughout the Westminster Standards

In previous chapters we have seen that when the debate about active obedience was directly before the Westminster Assembly—in 1643 when it was revising the Thirty-Nine Articles—it clearly chose to affirm this doctrine. It has also been noted that we have no record of any debate over active obedience whatsoever *after* that 1643 debate—that is, there was no direct debate about active obedience at the time of the adoption of the confession and catechisms. Does this mean that the earlier defenders of active obedience abandoned the field and no longer valued its affirmation? No, there is no reason to think that the Assembly strongly affirmed active obedience in 1643 and then came to disavow it in later years. I would argue that there was no further debate over the affirmation of active obedience because there was no need for such. It had earlier been affirmed in a debate that, of necessity, focused narrowly on the issue, because originally the only apparent way to affirm active obedience was to modify article 11 of the Thirty-Nine Articles.

When the revision of the Thirty-Nine Articles was no longer in view and an entirely new confession and catechisms were in consideration, there was no reason to repeat that earlier debate, because the Westminster Standards as a whole accorded far greater opportunity and space to express affirmation of active obedience in its several parts than in one particular article as it had in 1643. I contend that this greater space given to the expression of theology in the Westminster Standards permitted a fuller treatment of active obedience and allied matters and that there is in fact such a fuller, though not explicit, expression of such found within the Westminster Standards.[1]

The Westminster Confession of Faith

Let us begin with the confession of faith before proceeding to the catechisms. The first two chapters of the confession deal with Scripture and God (the Holy Trinity). In chapter 2 of the confession we see, first of all, that God is holy and requires that His creatures be holy (which is what active obedience is all about):

> There is but one only, living, and true God, who is infinite in being and perfection, a most pure spirit, invisible, without body, parts, or passions; immutable, immense, eternal, incomprehensible, almighty, most wise, most holy, most free, most absolute;

---

1. While rarely quoting from them, this chapter is indebted to the treatment of the Westminster Standards by David Dickson, A. A. Hodge, Thomas Ridgeley, Robert Shaw, Chad Van Dixhoorn, J. G. Vos, and G. I. Williamson.

working all things according to the counsel of his own immutable and most righteous will, for his own glory; most loving, gracious, merciful, long-suffering, abundant in goodness and truth, forgiving iniquity, transgression, and sin; the rewarder of them that diligently seek him; and withal, most just, and terrible in his judgments, hating all sin, and who will by no means clear the guilty. (WCF 2.1)

This God, equally righteous and loving, hates sin and will not clear the guilty. How will sinful man then be saved? This is part of the theological setup in the confession for the reason that Christ's keeping the whole law must be imputed to us. The end of WCF 2.2 makes clear the requirement for perfect obedience that befits such a holy God: "He is most holy in all his counsels, in all his works, and in all his commands. To him is due from angels and men, and every other creature, whatsoever worship, service, or obedience he is pleased to require of them."

Chapter 3, in treating God's eternal decree, sets forth God's salvation plan in broad terms. Central to what God has decreed is the salvation of the elect "in Christ, unto everlasting glory, out of his mere free grace and love, without any foresight of faith, or good works, or perseverance in either of them, or any other thing in the creature" (3.5). Nothing meritorious in the elect qualifies them for salvation. Rather, "they who are elected, being fallen in Adam, are redeemed by Christ, are effectually called unto faith in Christ by his Spirit working in due season, are justified, adopted, sanctified, and kept by his power, through faith, unto salvation" (3.6). If the elect are justified (i.e., declared to be righteous) but have no inherent righteousness after the fall, they must have righteousness *accredited* to them as part of their justification; otherwise, God would be declaring something false to be true (that sinners are righteous when they are not). This is the seed of the doctrine of active obedience in our justification that is crucial to the system of doctrine contained in the Westminster Standards.

Chapter 4 of the confession addresses creation, including male and female as its crown:

> After God had made all the other creatures, he created man, male and female, with reasonable and immortal souls, endued with knowledge, righteousness, and true holiness, after his own image; having the law of God written in their hearts, and power to fulfill it: and yet under a possibility of transgressing, being left to the liberty of their own will, which was subject unto change. Beside this law written in their hearts, they received a command, not to eat of the tree of the knowledge of good and evil; which while they kept, they were happy in their communion with God, and had dominion over the creatures. (4.2)

This is worth quoting fully because it sets the prelapsarian plate for us: man was created as a law-creature, endowed with the power to fulfill the law (to keep the covenant of works), having it written in his heart. To put it another way, by God's gracious creational provision man had the ability to engage in active obedience (to keep the law that God gave him) and thus successfully to surmount the probation implied in WCF 4.2.

Man's state before the fall, in which he had the ability to keep the law and please God, was holy and happy. Having set forth creation in WCF 4 (the work of the first six days, the fulfilling in time and space of the first part of God's decrees), in WCF 5 the divines address providence, which is the fulfilling of God's decrees in the rest of history. Sin, and the problem of evil, as part of God's providence, is first addressed here:

> The almighty power, unsearchable wisdom, and infinite goodness of God so far manifest themselves in his providence, that it extendeth itself even to the first fall, and all other sins of angels and men; and that not by a bare permission, but such as hath joined with it a most wise and powerful bounding, and otherwise ordering, and governing of them, in a manifold dispensation, to his own holy ends; yet so, as the sinfulness thereof proceedeth only from the creature, and not from God, who, being most holy and righteous, neither is nor can be the author or approver of sin. (5.4)

This makes clear that sin comes not from God but from the creature, who had "power to fulfill" the law as well as the "possibility of transgressing." Thus, man failed in his first task: to fulfill the law and thereby to continue, and even be confirmed, in the favor of God. Man, by his own fault, failed to continue in active obedience as God had commanded and enabled him.

Chapter 6 of the confession fleshes this out as it speaks "Of the Fall of Man, of Sin, and of the Punishment Thereof." Section 1 says, "Our first parents, being seduced by the subtilty and temptation of Satan, sinned, in eating the forbidden fruit. This their sin, God was pleased, according to his wise and holy counsel, to permit, having purposed to order it to his own glory." Adam and Eve's sin, something that was their fault and for which they were fully responsible (seen in WCF 5.4), was something permitted by God for His own glory. This is a most curious statement if God did not intend to do something to set right what Adam fouled up. God, being righteous (seen in WCF 2.1), cannot bring glory to Himself by ignoring or overlooking what Adam has done. If God is to bring such glory, He must do so in a way that ensures He is just as well as the justifier of man, who has become a sinner.

The rest of WCF 6 proceeds to describe the horrible effects of the fall for Adam and Eve and "all their posterity descending from them by ordinary generation." The guilt of Adam's first sin, the corruption of his whole nature, and the loss of original righteousness and communion with God are inherited by his biological descendants and imputed to the human race. Man, who had been blessed before the fall, now becomes cursed: "Every sin, both original and actual, being a transgression of the righteous law of God, and contrary thereunto, doth, in its own nature, bring guilt upon the sinner, whereby he is bound over to the wrath of God, and curse of the law, and so made subject to death, with all miseries spiritual, temporal, and eternal" (6.6).

Following its opening chapters on Scripture, God, the decrees, creation, providence, and the fall of man, the Westminster Confession of Faith comes to address God's covenant with man. Although this treatment of covenant does not occur until WCF 7, after other important theological topics have been addressed, this does not mean that the notion of covenant was in any sense marginal to the theological construct that the Westminster divines sought to set forth. Quite to the contrary, the doctrine of covenant assumes a large role in the structure of the confession and catechisms. This is evident in the first section of WCF 7, which seeks to address the challenging question of how God, given the sort of infinite, eternal being that He is, could ever have any meaningful relationship with man, a mere finite being: "The distance between God and the creature is so great, that although reasonable creatures do owe obedience unto him as their Creator, yet they could never have any fruition of him as their blessedness and reward, but by some voluntary condescension on God's part, which he hath been pleased to express by way of covenant."

This "voluntary condescension on God's part" means that God, by an act of His sovereign and free will, determined to enter into the kind of relationship with His creature that involved not merely duty (as reasonable creatures owing Him obedience) but entailed a knowledge of and relationship with Him involving blessedness and reward. Thus, we might say that God created man and entered into this relationship with him, which was defined and expressed by way of covenant. This means that covenant was an integral part of God's creation of man. We might even say that covenant is a particularly fitting way for a loving and just God to interact with His reasonable creatures (as opposed to the lower creation, which would not be designated as "reasonable creatures"). But covenant was a voluntary act (i.e., a free act of the will) on God's part; indeed, it involved a condescension on His part—a "coming down," given His ontological status (as God) to us in our ontological status (as creatures).

Section 2 then proceeds to tell us what God's initial covenant with man involved: "The first covenant made with man was a covenant of works, wherein life was promised to Adam; and in him to his posterity, upon condition of perfect and personal obedience." Man's initial condition at his creation was in the context of a covenantal relationship that involved a promise: if he continued in perfect and personal obedience, the reward for him and his posterity would be life. Since Adam already had life, clearly this promise was an eschatological one that entailed a confirmation and continuation in life that he did not then possess. By good and necessary consequence, then, if Adam was promised some sort of life that he did not then possess on the terms of a condition (perfect and personal obedience), this means that Adam was placed in a state of probation, a circumstance in which the condition of his being confirmed in life would be tested.

This reality of a probation for man in the covenant of works is also addressed in chapter 9 of the confession, which treats the matter of free will. Section 1, first of all, asserts that man has free will in this fashion: "God hath endued the will of man with that natural liberty, that it is neither forced, nor, by any absolute necessity of nature, determined to good, or evil." Particularly, man in his first estate—which is to say man in the covenant of works, in the time of his innocency—had freedom and ability to obey God, to continue through all circumstances (through any sort of test or probation) in personal and perfect obedience. Such freedom involves the contrary power as well: the freedom not only to obey but also not to obey. Section 2 of chapter 9 puts it this way: "Man, in his state of innocency, had freedom, and power to will and to do that which was good and well pleasing to God; but yet, mutably, so that he might fall from it."

We note here the saddest truth of history (next to the death of our Lord, to which this reality led): man did not retain his estate. He did not pass the probation but rather fell into sin by willfully disobeying God. Section 3 speaks of the consequences of the fall, especially pertaining to man's will: "Man, by his fall into a state of sin, hath wholly lost all ability of will to any spiritual good accompanying salvation: so as, a natural man, being altogether averse from that good, and dead in sin, is not able, by his own strength, to convert himself, or to prepare himself thereunto." In other words, man, by his fall, has violated the terms of that initial covenant of works and has rendered himself incapable of life by keeping its terms.

Returning to WCF 7.3, which addresses man's failure in the covenant of works and God's remedy for such in the covenant of grace, we read: "Man, by his fall, having made himself incapable of life by that covenant [the covenant of works], the Lord was pleased to make a second, commonly called the covenant of grace; wherein he freely offereth unto sinners life and salvation by Jesus Christ; requiring of them faith in him, that they may be saved, and promising to give unto all those that are ordained unto eternal life his Holy Spirit, to make them willing, and able to believe." So in failing to maintain the terms of the covenant of works ("perfect and personal obedience"), man thus failed to attain to the eternal life promised to him in it. God would have been wholly just in judging man then and there and condemning him to eternal death. But He did not. Out of His mercy, grace, and love, God was pleased (again, as an act of His free and sovereign will) to make a second covenant with man—a covenant of grace—whereby man, now a miserable sinner, could gain life, not under the terms of the first covenant, which he had already forfeited, but under the terms of a second (faith in Jesus Christ).[2]

---

2. In fact, WLC 31, in answer to the question "With whom was the covenant of grace made?" answers, "The covenant of grace was made with Christ as the second Adam, and in him with all the elect as his seed." That this covenant was made not with man but with Christ highlights that it is Christ who will keep all its terms and fulfill it. His

Once man had fallen into sin, life was no longer held forth in the covenant of works, which can only condemn him now. Those who remain outside of Christ remain in the covenant of works, and thus eternal death will be the consequence of that violated covenant. This is why Paul says that "in Adam all die." All those who died in Adam and remain in him, never coming to Christ, abide in death and will ultimately be cast into the lake of fire. Those who are "in Christ" are "made alive" since "by man [Adam] came death, by man [Christ] came also the resurrection of the dead" (1 Cor. 15:21–22). How? By Christ coming and keeping the covenant of works for us that Adam violated. As noted earlier, for Christ the covenant of grace was a covenant of works, which He kept perfectly for us. Even as the guilt of Adam's first sin has been imputed to us, so now is Christ's righteousness in His keeping covenant perfectly for us (Rom. 5:12–28). This is the structure of covenant as found in the Westminster Standards.

Chapter 8 of the confession now turns our focus to the mediator of the covenant of grace and His divine rescue mission. Adam has violated the covenant of works and plunged the human race into ruin and misery. We have been told, from the point of view of God and His decrees, that all will be set right and redound to His glory. But how is it to be done? Enter the subject matter of

---

doing so is the essence of His active obedience: done not for Himself but for us and imputed to us.

WCF 8, "Of Christ the Mediator." Sections 1 and 2 read as follows:

> 8.1: It pleased God, in his eternal purpose, to choose and ordain the Lord Jesus, his only begotten Son, to be the Mediator between God and man, the Prophet, Priest, and King, the Head and Savior of his church, the Heir of all things, and Judge of the world: unto whom he did from all eternity give a people, to be his seed, and to be by him in time redeemed, called, justified, sanctified, and glorified.

> 8.2: The Son of God, the second person in the Trinity, being very and eternal God, of one substance and equal with the Father, did, when the fullness of time was come, take upon him man's nature, with all the essential properties, and common infirmities thereof, yet without sin; being conceived by the power of the Holy Ghost, in the womb of the virgin Mary, of her substance. So that two whole, perfect, and distinct natures, the Godhead and the manhood, were inseparably joined together in one person, without conversion, composition, or confusion. Which person is very God, and very man, yet one Christ, the only Mediator between God and man.

Sections 1 and 2, together with Section 3, define the person of Christ. Section 4 goes on to describe His work, which says in part, "He was made under the law, and did perfectly fulfill it; endured most grievous torments immediately in his soul, and most painful sufferings in his body; was crucified, and died, was buried, and remained under the power of death." This, by any fair reading, would refer

to both His active and passive obedience, with the active
being in view especially in the words "made under the law,
and did perfectly fulfill it." One may object, as some have,
that Christ's fulfilling of the law was merely to qualify
Him to be a sinless sacrifice; others have averred that, as
a man, Christ was obliged at any rate to keep the law.[3]
However, it is the case that Christ, in the integrity of His
theanthropic person, was under no obligation whatsoever to keep the law for Himself. As God, He was not
subject to the law in the same way as the creature. When
the law giver became the law keeper, He did so *pro nobis*,
as He did when He suffered the cruel death of the cross.
He lived for us, rendering perfect obedience to the law at
every point in our stead, as well as suffered and died for
us, yielding His life, enduring the death that we deserve
for our sin.

The whole of His life and death was in solidarity
with us, representative of us, and substitutionary for us.
This is the particular import of the phrase that begins
WCF 8.4: "This office the Lord Jesus did most willingly
undertake." A recent study committee of the Orthodox Presbyterian Church (OPC) commentated on this
phrase and what it implies:

> The first aspect of a properly meritorious work (a
> work deserving of reward) is that it is free. If one
> must perform a work as a matter of debt, he or she

---

3. E.g., Daniel Kirk and Norman Shepherd. See note 1 in chapter 1
of this work.

can hardly request a reward for that work when completed. Under this heading, as in every aspect of a discussion of merit, we encounter a contrast between ourselves and our Savior. Such is our debt to the one who has made us and rules over us, such is the relationship of man to his maker, that as reasoning "creatures" we "owe obedience unto" God as our "Creator" (WCF 7.1). Indeed, quite apart from the fact that we "are guilty both of original and actual sin, and thereby [have] become debtors to the justice of God" (LC 194), every one of us knows that we owe "whatsoever worship, service, or obedience he is pleased to require of" us (WCF 2:2). But Jesus Christ, by way of contrast, is no mere creature and he owed no obedience to the creator. This was a subject about which the assembly debated at length, and thus the gathering's statement that the incarnate "Lord Jesus did most willingly undertake" his work as our mediator should be read as a deliberate and not an accidental comment on his meritorious work (WCF 8.4). His actions were performed freely, and not as a matter of debt. His work was meritorious because it was free.[4]

Section 4 thus implies that Christ did what He did for us: the merit of His whole obedience is imputed to

---

4. "The Report of the Committee to Study Republication of the General Assembly of the Orthodox Presbyterian Church," in *Minutes of the 83rd General Assembly of the Orthodox Presbyterian Church* (2016), 364–65. It is important to note the footnote substantiating the claim that "this was a subject about which the Assembly debated at length." Van Dixhoorn, *Minutes*, 2:48–107 (Sess. 47–52; Sept. 6–12, 1643). This and other places in this important report would tend to confirm that the Assembly affirmed active obedience.

us, and thus active obedience is affirmed. Perhaps active obedience is made even clearer in WCF 8.5: "The Lord Jesus, by his perfect obedience, and sacrifice of himself, which he, through the eternal Spirit, once offered up unto God, hath fully satisfied the justice of his Father; and purchased, not only reconciliation, but an everlasting inheritance in the kingdom of heaven, for all those whom the Father hath given unto him." I contend, as do a number of other scholars treating this passage, that this affirms both the active and passive obedience of Christ. The perfect obedience refers to His life of completely and entirely keeping the law for us, a life lived in our place and for us: this is the active obedience of Christ, coupled with His sacrifice of Himself, which refers to His passive obedience. These, taken together and as a package, constitute Christ's whole obedience (in keeping with what the Assembly affirmed in September 1643) and have the net effect of fully satisfying the offended justice of God due to our sinfulness.

Given that the Westminster divines, when discussing revisions to article 11 of the Thirty-Nine Articles in 1643 (the article treating justification), chose to affirm the active obedience of Christ clearly by adopting the words *whole obedience*, and given that there is no evidence whatsoever of a subsequent alteration of that view, it seems most reasonable to conclude that the divines continued to hold such a view and to give expression to it as appropriate in the Westminster Standards. Previously, the divines were confined to expressing in the limited space of a single article the entirety of their views respecting the matter of active obedience. But once the divines determined to jettison revising the Thirty-Nine Articles in favor of writing a new confession altogether (obviously necessary after entering into the Solemn League and Covenant with the Scots), the affirmation of the imputation of Christ's active obedience could find wider expression. It is my contention that it did, as we have seen, in theology proper, anthropology, and particularly in Christology, in which Christ's work as mediator is said, conclusively, to consist of two parts: His perfect obedience and His sacrifice of Himself.

It is hardly unsurprising that the divines did not choose to repeat the debate over the word *whole* as a qualifier of *obedience*, in either the Christology section that we have just reviewed or the soteriology section that we shall shortly examine. That debate had been waged and won, and, as is not unusual for a deliberative body, it was not reengaged when thought unnecessary. The divines had many ways at their disposal to express a continuing affirmation of active obedience and, I believe, did so without needing to revisit the 1643 debate and its word choices. It is clear, even as we survey the confession on its doctrine of the Holy Spirit and of salvation, that the divines did not specifically revisit the debates of 1643. But this hardly means that they failed to affirm active obedience in our justification.

There is no known reason why they would fail to do so in 1646–1647 when they did it in 1643, especially in light of the death of the prolocutor of the Westminster

Assembly, William Twisse, in July 1646. Twisse, although moderator of the Assembly, was a known primary opponent of the phrase *whole obedience* back in 1643, but he was no longer around when the relevant portions of the WCF were adopted by the Assembly. If the Assembly refused to accommodate Twisse when he was alive, it seems highly unlikely that it would do so after his death. Thus, we have no reason to believe that what the Assembly affirmed over Twisse's objections when he was alive was then reversed and affirmed otherwise after his death.

Continuing on in the confession, then, the treatment of man in his fourfold state (WCF 9) has implications for active obedience with respect to the overall federal theology of the confession, which has already received treatment in its most relevant part in our discussion of WCF 7 above. The next obvious focus is WCF 11 on justification. Those whom God effectually calls, He "freely" justifies, "by pardoning their sins, and by accounting and accepting their persons as righteous" (11.1). No one since the fall is corporately (or federally) righteous (being guilty of Adam's first sin by imputation) or personally righteous (being guilty of our own sins, having inherited a corrupt sin nature). So those whom God justifies (those called and regenerated) are, in fact, sinners, and God both pardons their sins and accounts them to be righteous. This raises what John Murray calls the great religious question: On what basis can God regard sinners as righteous, being, as He is, the God of truth? And the answer is given here in WCF 11.1: God does not justify by "infusing righteousness" (contra Rome) nor "for anything wrought in them or done by them" (including faith itself or "any other evangelical obedience"), but God justifies solely "by imputing the obedience and satisfaction of Christ unto them." This pardon and righteousness is received by faith alone, which itself is a gift of God, not something self-produced. Every possible trace of auto-soteriology (or self-salvation) is hereby denied.

Further affirmation of active obedience may be found in WCF 11.3: "Christ, by his obedience and death, did fully discharge the debt of all those that are thus justified, and did make a proper, real, and full satisfaction to his Father's justice in their behalf. Yet, inasmuch as he was given by the Father for them; and his obedience and satisfaction accepted in their stead; and both, freely, not for anything in them; their justification is only of free grace; that both the exact justice and rich grace of God might be glorified in the justification of sinners." Several things are noteworthy here in the support of the doctrine of active obedience. The first sentence again speaks of not only Christ's death but His "obedience and death," asserting that He "fully" discharged the debt (which consists of the requirement both to keep the law and to pay for any transgressions of it).[5] This obedience and death

---

5. John Fesko finds it significant that the original 1647 text of the WCF (in contrast to the more commonly used Carruthers edition produced in the twentieth century) has an additional comma in 11.3 separating *obedience* and *death*: "Christ, by his *obedience, and death,* did fully discharge." He argues that the comma serves to distinguish

made a "proper, real, and full satisfaction" to God's "justice." Again, the full language suggests whole obedience, both passive and active obedience, to satisfy justice. And the phrase in the second sentence, "his [Jesus'] obedience and satisfaction accepted in their stead," suggests even further active obedience: the "in our stead" means "in our place, on our behalf, for us," intimating that Christ was our substitute not only in death (satisfaction) but also in life (obedience).

Further clues to the affirmation of active obedience lie in the chapters on good works and the perseverance of the saints (WCF 16–17). In WCF 16, justified persons (who are also adopted and being sanctified, including ongoing faith and repentance) can confidently do good works, even knowing that such works "are defiled, and mixed with so much weakness and imperfection, that they cannot endure the severity of God's judgment" (16.5). They can perform such good works, imperfect though they may be, because "the persons of believers being accepted through Christ, their good works also are accepted in him" (16.6). This means that believers, being justified by the obedience and satisfaction of Christ (including active obedience), have a perfect standing with God and thus can offer less than perfect works and have the Father joyfully accept them "although accompanied with many weaknesses and imperfections" (16.6). WCF 17 explicitly

"two separate aspects of Christ's work," reflecting both "the passive *and* active obedience" (all emphases original). *Theology of the Westminster Standards*, 225.

affirms that the perseverance of the Christian is certain because of a number of things, including the "efficacy of the merit and intercession of Jesus Christ" (17.2), another nod to active obedience.

The chapter on the law of God (WCF 19) fits in well with the discussion of covenant theology, as do the chapters on covenant (WCF 7) and free will (WCF 9).[6] Chapter 19 ties the law of God into the covenants both of works and grace, showing the role that it plays in each. Section 1 asserts, "God gave to Adam a law, as a covenant of works, by which he bound him and all his posterity to personal, entire, exact, and perpetual obedience, promised life upon the fulfilling, and threatened death upon the breach of it, and endued him with power and ability to keep it." So the law, as a revelation of God's perfect character, was set before man in his first estate as that which he was bound, able, and empowered to keep, yielding eternal life upon uncompromising obedience (the obedience must be "personal, entire, exact, and perpetual") and threatening destruction for disobedience.

But man's violation of the law, as devastating as that was, did not end or destroy the law. Section 2 notes, "This law, after his fall, continued to be a perfect rule of righteousness; and, as such, was delivered by God upon Mount Sinai, in ten commandments, and written in two tables: the first four commandments containing our duty

------

6. See the previous discussion in this chapter and also in chapter 7 of this work.

towards God; and the other six, our duty to man." The
law continued to be in full force, although man by his sin
had transgressed it. God continued to hold it forth and
require it of man, especially in the Ten Commandments
as a summary of the law—God's will concerning our duty
to Him and to our fellow man. The law given at Sinai was
simply a blossoming of the seed given to Adam and Eve
in the garden. Sections 3 and 4 note that in addition to
this moral law (summarized in the Ten Commandments),
God gave laws allied to it that were particularly for His
people in their time of tutelage: the ceremonial and judicial laws given to Israel that have been abrogated or have
expired in the New Testament expression of the covenant
of grace. In other words, Christ came and fulfilled all the
ceremonial laws, and the judicial laws were for the church
in the time of its youth.

As for the moral law, Christ fulfilled it (WCF 19.6)
along with the ceremonial and judicial laws, for the salvation of the elect. The fifth section of chapter 19 makes it
clear, however, that the moral law, unlike the ceremonial
and judicial, continues to bind all, including the justified, giving no quarter to the antinomian teaching that
the justified were not bound to keep the moral law: "The
moral law doth forever bind all, as well justified persons
as others, to the obedience thereof; and that, not only in
regard of the matter contained in it, but also in respect of
the authority of God the Creator, who gave it. Neither
doth Christ, in the gospel, any way dissolve, but much
strengthen this obligation." It is also especially important

when affirming active obedience to assert that Christ's having kept the law for us does not free His children from keeping the law for Him, out of gratitude, as the proper expression of the fruit and evidence of our faith. Section 6 of chapter 19 expands on the use of the moral law as a guide for Christians (the "third use of the law"), speaking of the law playing a variety of instructive roles for the Christian, including the provision of "a clearer sight of the need they have of Christ, and the perfection of his obedience" (suggesting active obedience as well as passive).

Proceeding to the next chapter, WCF 20.1 notes that the liberty of the Christian consists in their freedom, among other things, "from the guilt of sin, the condemning wrath of God, [and] the curse of the moral law." The moral law curses all who break it, and the only way that it cannot curse is for the law to be kept. This is what Christ did for us, and it is what active obedience is all about. The guilt of sin (expiation) and the condemning wrath of God (propitiation) are removed in the atoning death of Christ. The curse of the moral law is removed by Christ's keeping it for us. While the remainder of the confession of faith may have expressions here and there that indirectly reflect active obedience, we have looked at the most important of them, especially in our survey of God, man, Christ, and soteriology.

The Catechisms

There are also a host of Westminster Larger Catechism (WLC) and Westminster Shorter Catechism (WSC) questions and answers that impact the matter of active obedience in these standards. We will restrict our treatment here to the WLC (and largely to citing and not quoting because the dogma is thought to be contained largely in the WCF) since it is to a great degree inclusive of the WSC, and the latter has received many treatments. In WLC 17 we are told that male and female were in creation, made to be law creatures: "having the law of God written in their hearts." This was part and parcel of their being, before the fall, in a "covenant of life" (WLC 20; another way of speaking of the covenant of works). WLC 21 notes that Adam and Eve sinned, causing the fall of all mankind (WLC 22) and bringing man into an estate of misery (WLC 23). Original sin (WLC 25) is defined as the guilt of Adam's first sin, the want of original righteousness, and the total corruption of his nature; WLC 26 notes that this original sin is conveyed "from our first parents to their posterity by natural generation" so that the whole of humanity is hereafter conceived and born in sin (excepting Christ, who was not born of ordinary generation). Questions 28–29 address the punishment due for sin, here and hereafter. All of this has implications for why Christ will need to come to keep the law that neither Adam nor we have kept.

WLC 30 shifts our focus to the covenant of grace. Man has failed in the covenant of works, and the way of life by his own keeping of that covenant is not open to him. Thus, God makes a covenant of grace with Adam and in him His elect seed (WLC 31), manifesting the wonder of His grace (WLC 32). WLC 33–35 speak of the different ways that this one covenant of grace was administered under the Old and New Testaments. In this covenant of grace, Christ serves as mediator (WLC 36), being both God (WLC 38) and man (WLC 39) in that mediatorial work, those questions highlighting the necessity for the mediator to be God and man. Part of what Jesus' divinity bestowed on His mediatorial work was to "give worth and efficacy to his sufferings, obedience, and his intercession" (WLC 38), which comes close to saying passive obedience ("sufferings and intercession") and active obedience ("obedience").

Even more explicitly, perhaps as much so as anywhere in the Westminster Standards, WLC 39 says that it was requisite that the mediator should be man, "that he might advance our nature, [and] perform obedience to the law." This last phrase, "perform obedience to the law," is what Christ did in His active obedience that is imputed to us in our justification. The proof texts for both of these phrases are Hebrews 2:16 and 2 Peter 1:4 (for "advance our nature") and Galatians 4:4, Matthew 5:17, Romans 5:19, and Philippians 2:8 (for "perform obedience to the law"), all keys texts for those who affirm active obedience. I realize that all of this can be read in a more minimalistic fashion, but the Assembly did not read it that way in September 1643, and there is no reason to believe that it is here excluding active obedience in what the divines are affirming.

WLC 41–42 specifically identify the mediator as Jesus Christ, proceeding to set forth His threefold office (WLC 43–45) and twofold estates of humiliation and exaltation (WLC 46–56) and the work pertaining thereunto. WLC 48 addresses the matter of Christ's humbling Himself in this life, noting that He did so, in part, "by subjecting himself to the law, which he perfectly fulfilled," different from the humiliation that He suffered in death (WLC 49). WLC 48 clearly affirms Christ's active obedience. WLC 52 notes that the resurrection testifies, among other things, to Christ "[having] satisfied divine justice… which he did as a public person, the head of his church, for their justification." This ties together satisfaction of justice (which requires the keeping of the law and, in the case of violation, the payment of due penalty—thus the active and passive obedience of Christ) and justification. Christ's active as well as passive obedience was necessary to satisfy divine justice for our justification.

WLC 55 is also rather explicit here in affirming that Christ makes intercession for us "by his appearing in our nature continually before the Father in heaven, in the merit of his obedience and sacrifice on earth, declaring his will to have it applied to all believers; answering all accusations against them, and procuring for them quiet of conscience, notwithstanding daily failings, access with boldness to the throne of grace, and acceptance of their persons and services." The language of merit suggests that Christ did this for us, not for Himself. (Why would He need to merit anything with His Father?) We are the ones who have de-merited God's favor because of sin, meriting only God's wrath; Jesus did not need to win the Father's favor but ever has it as the beloved in whom the Father is well pleased. His obedience and sacrifice (active and passive obedience) on earth were for us (it is applied— imputed—to all His children). Thus, our persons and services enjoy acceptance, all because Christ took our nature, doing what we (and Adam) failed to do (keep the law) and undoing what we did (breaking the law in all points), all of this being graciously applied to all believers. WLC 55 has many elements that strongly support active obedience.

The WLC finishes its treatment of Christology and proceeds to its doctrine of the Holy Spirit (speaking also here of the visible and invisible church), specifically linking Christology and Pneumatology in several questions, especially WLC 69, which speaks of the elect (members of the invisible church) becoming partakers "of the virtue of [Christ's] mediation, in their justification…and whatever else, in this life, manifests their union with him." The Holy Spirit is the agent who brings us to Christ and Christ to us. Regarding justification, the whole of WLC 70 deserves quoting: "Justification is an act of God's free grace unto sinners, in which he pardoneth all their sins, accepteth and accounteth their persons righteous in his sight; not for anything wrought in them, or done by them, but only for the perfect obedience and full satisfaction of Christ, by God imputed to them, and received by faith alone."

Here it is put in even fuller terms: "perfect obedience and full satisfaction of Christ." Full satisfaction would comprehend all of Christ's suffering, culminating in His atoning death. Perfect obedience would have in view His keeping of the whole law. And all of that, both the perfect obedience and full satisfaction that is imputed to us, would have in view that both Christ's active and passive obedience were for us rather than in any sense for Himself. WLC 71, in addressing how it is that justification is an act of God's free grace, notes that "Christ, by his obedience and death, did make a proper, real, and full satisfaction to God's justice in the behalf of them that are justified," again mentioning obedience and death, not just His death.

WLC 71 goes on to note that this justification is accomplished not by anything that the sinner does but only because of what his surety does: "God accepteth the satisfaction from a surety, which he might have demanded of them, and did provide this surety, his own only Son, imputing his righteousness to them, and requiring nothing of them for their justification but faith, which also is his gift, their justification is to them of free grace." This further highlights that Christ acted globally as the substitute for the elect sinner, not only in His death but also in His life.

As we saw in chapter 3 of this work, WLC 72 makes it clear that justifying faith is entirely extraspective, relying on nothing in the subject but looking to and trusting in Christ and His righteousness as the sole ground of justification and exclusive object of faith. And WLC 73 affirms that this faith, as far as justification is in view, is the sole instrument for receiving Christ and His righteousness. Note that it is always "Christ and his righteousness," consisting of His whole obedience, rendered in His active and passive obedience, imputed to His people for their justification.

After the extended section on the Holy Spirit, the WLC proceeds to treat the doctrine of the Christian life under the rubric of the Ten Commandments. WLC 92–93 note that the moral law of God is His rule for obedience, introduced in Eden before the fall, "directing and binding everyone to personal, perfect, and perpetual conformity and obedience thereunto, in the frame and disposition of the whole man, soul, and body, and in performance of all those duties of holiness and righteousness which he oweth to God and man: promising life upon the fulfilling, and threatening death upon the breach of it" (WLC 93). This affirmation of "life upon the fulfilling" of the moral law suggests that some sort of eschatological reward not yet in his possession awaited Adam upon his fulfillment of the rule he had been given in Eden. Adam had life, yet he was promised life of some greater sort, presumably, upon a successful probation. The breach would bring death. This suggests that Christ came not only to repair the breach of the broken law but actually to fulfill it. In other words, He came to deliver us from death in His passive obedience (imputed to us) and to bring us (by the imputation of His active obedience to the law) into the life promised to but never achieved by Adam.

WLC 95 addresses the use of the moral law to all men: "The moral law is of use to all men, to inform them of the holy nature and will of God, and of their duty, binding them to walk accordingly; to convince them of their disability to keep it, and of the sinful pollution of their nature, hearts, and lives: to humble them in the sense of their sin and misery, and thereby help them to a clearer sight of the need they have of Christ, and of the perfection of his obedience." Taken together, this means that man, although bound to obey the moral law, has no ability to keep it after the fall, and such inability heightens the sense of the need of the perfection of Christ's obedience.

Clearly, such obedience is not chiefly exemplary but is rendered on behalf of those who are required to provide such but cannot. This further supports that the WLC affirms active obedience, as does WLC 97 (in addressing the special use of the moral law to the regenerate): "[The moral law] is of special use, to show [the regenerate] how much they are bound to Christ for his fulfilling it, and enduring the curse thereof in their stead, and for their good." This statement clearly affirms that Christ fulfilled the moral law on behalf of the elect, who are thus "bound to Christ for his fulfilling it...in their stead." Christ not only endured the curse "in their stead" but fulfilled the moral law "in their stead." This seems incontrovertible evidence of the affirmation of active obedience.

After the lengthy section on the Ten Commandments, the WLC proceeds to address the means of grace (Word, sacraments, and prayer). WLC 174, addressing the conduct of believers at the Lord's Table, notes that they should receive the sacrament, among other things, "trusting in his merits," giving as a proof text Philippians 3:9, which contrasts our own righteousness through our law-keeping with faith in Christ as the one who has kept the law perfectly for us. Finally, in the WLC's section on prayer, we are told in WLC 193 that as sinners, we merit nothing but judgment, and in WLC 194 that we cannot make the "least satisfaction" for our sin, but that God has "through the obedience and satisfaction of Christ." WLC 195 again emphasizes our inability, while the last question, WLC 196, notes that there is no worthiness in us but only and entirely in God.

More could be said, but we are safe to assert that the Westminster Standards clearly tend to affirm the imputation of Christ's active obedience to us for our justification.

Active Obedience and Federal Theology

In broader evangelical theology in the post–World War II era, active obedience has not played a prominent role in our doctrine of justification; it often has been eclipsed, if not altogether pushed out, by the doctrine of the passive obedience of Christ. This is due, in no small measure, to the role that active obedience plays in the theology of the covenant,[1] or federal theology, which itself fell on hard times in the twentieth century. If active obedience is particularly connected to federal theology (as demonstrated by men such as Francis Turretin, Charles Hodge, and Herman Bavinck),[2] and if federal theology has been on the decline, then it is unsurprising that the doctrine of active obedience has receded into the background. To recover it, we need to recover federal theology. Perhaps we should examine something of the difficult days that federal theology has endured, particularly in

---

1. As set forth in chapter 6 of this work.
2. See the references to these in the introduction of this work.

the last century, as we seek to bring it back into favor in Reformed and Presbyterian circles.

The Treatment of Covenant Theology

We say that the theology given expression in the Westminster Standards is federal theology, or a theology given shape and definition by the covenants—namely, the covenants of works and grace explicitly and, some would add, the covenant of redemption implicitly. Much controversy has arisen with respect to the doctrine of the covenants taught in the standards.[3] The controversy is not over whether the standards espouse a federal theology (*federal* is from the Latin word for "covenant"—*foedus*); it is rather widely agreed that the standards do embody such federalism. The controversy involves questions over whether the federalism of the Westminster Standards differs from the sixteenth-century Reformed theology of Calvin, Zwingli, Bullinger, and others, and, if so, if it is properly progressive or regressive.[4] I would argue that there is essential

---

3. The basic doctrine of the covenants is set forth in the treatment of the Westminster Confession of Faith in chapter 6 of this work.

4. For surveys and critical assessments of various approaches to the interpretation of Calvin's theology, including the "two traditions" thesis, see Wilhelm Niesel, *The Theology of Calvin* (Philadelphia: Westminster Press, 1956), 9–21; Richard Muller, *After Calvin: Studies in the Development of a Theological Tradition* (New York: Oxford University Press, 1993), 63–80; Richard Muller, "Directions in Current Calvin Research," *Religious Studies Review* 27, no. 2 (2002): 131–38; Cornelis P. Venema, *Accepted and Renewed in Christ: The "Twofold Grace of God" and the Interpretation of Calvin's Theology* (Göttingen: Vandenhoeck & Ruprecht, 2007), 14–16; Cornelis P. Venema, *Heinrich Bullinger and*

continuity between Calvin and the Calvinists and that where they differ, Calvinism has represented a salubrious advance from Calvin.[5]

To take two exemplars of this "Calvin vs. the Calvinists" (or "two traditions") approach, both Perry Miller, a leading mid-twentieth-century American literary scholar, and Karl Barth (along with J. B. Torrance and many other Barthians) have argued that federal theology—that which developed out of Calvin's teaching, especially among the British Puritans and in the *Nadere Reformatie*—is discontinuous with the teaching of Calvin himself. Miller and Barth differed on their assessments of such a departure, however: Miller thought covenant theology an improvement, while Barth found it a decidedly retrograde move. Miller, it should be noted, considered

---

the Doctrine of Predestination: Author of "the Other Reformed Tradition" (Grand Rapids: Baker Academic, 2002), esp. 24–32; J. Mark Beach, *Christ and the Covenant: Francis Turretin's Federal Theology as a Defense of the Doctrine of Grace* (Göttingen: Vandenhoeck & Ruprecht, 2007), 22–60; Lyle D. Bierma, "Federal Theology in the Sixteenth Century: Two Traditions," *Westminster Theological Journal* 44, no. 2 (Fall 1983): 304–21; and Richard C. Gamble, "Current Trends in Calvin Research, 1982–90," in *Calvinus Sacrae Scripturae Professor*, ed. Wilhelm H. Neuser (Grand Rapids: Eerdmans, 1994), 91–112.

5. Kenneth Stewart, *Ten Myths about Calvinism: Recovering the Breadth of the Reformed Tradition* (Downers Grove, Ill.: InterVarsity Press, 2011), 44–72, addresses the contention that "Calvin's view of predestination must be" that of all Calvinists, arguing that Calvin's writings contain some expressions about predestination that are fairly strident and that later Calvinism was more balanced and nuanced on the subject, reflected not only in the expression given to such at Dort but also in the Westminster Confession of Faith (esp. WCF 3).

Calvin disturbing—a wild predestinarian, whose voluntaristic view of God renders the deity almost fickle. Thus, the federal theology of the Puritans (the sort expressed in the Westminster Standards) permits both a binding of God and space for human freedom, both of which Miller deemed vastly relieving and an improvement over Calvin's more capricious God. Miller believed federal theology to be a more livable and workable Calvinism, without which it descends into a hyper-Calvinistic decretal train wreck.[6]

Conversely, Barth saw Calvin as maintaining a more dynamic and vibrant Christianity, while federal theology descends into a new scholasticism that straightjackets theology, fostering legalism and Phariseeism. Barth agreed that the idea of the covenant in some measure was present in Calvin and earlier Reformed theologians. He objected, however, to the turn that this took later in the sixteenth and seventeenth centuries and its confessional expression in the Westminster Standards, particularly the development of a prefall covenant of works and the place of conditionality in federal theology (as well as matters that predated Westminster, like the Synod of Dort's affirmation of particular redemption).[7]

---

6. On the covenant of grace, see Perry Miller, *The New England Mind: The Seventeenth Century* (Cambridge, Mass.: Harvard Belknap Press, 1939), 365–97.

7. Karl Barth, *Church Dogmatics*, vol. 4.1, *The Doctrine of Reconciliation* (Edinburgh: T&T Clark, 1956), 54–66.

Other Challenges to Federal Theology

Certainly, this federal theology was not restricted to the Westminster tradition but thrived in the Netherlands in the works of G. Voetius, J. Cocceius, H. Witsius, W. à Brakel, and others.[8] It was especially well represented in Calvin's Geneva in the later seventeenth century by Turretin and would be taken up in America, particularly in Princeton and represented in the theology of Hodge. However, it began to fall on hard times, even in the nineteenth century, before the misunderstanding of Miller and his followers and the contempt of Barth and Barthians. Ligon Duncan notes that the fears of John L. Girardeau proved prophetic when he warned that federal theology appeared imperiled in the nineteenth century and liable to rough sailing ahead. Duncan observes, "Under the incessant pounding of theological rationalism, popular evangelical Arminianism, advancing Dispensationalism, and the general reductionistic doctrinal trends of the age, the federal theology—as part of core teaching on the doctrines of salvation—fell into oblivion in the early part of the twentieth century (save as a prop for sacramental theology in Presbyterian circles)."[9]

Duncan notes the irony of evangelicals and Reformed Christians moving away from federal theology in the nineteenth and twentieth centuries while other scholars

---

8. Trevor A. Hart, ed., *Dictionary of Historical Theology* (Grand Rapids: Eerdmans, 2000), 131–33.

9. J. Ligon Duncan, "Recent Objections to Covenant Theology: A Description, Evaluation, and Response," in *The Westminster Confession into the 21st Century*, 3:467–500.

seemed to be discovering the covenant. Biblical scholars, especially those of the redemptive-historical schools
(both confessional and liberal), found the concept of the
covenant fecund, especially in the context of ancient Near
Eastern treaty making. This is not to say that the use of
the covenant idea made by everyone from Old and New
Testament scholars to "progressive" dispensationalists
and liberation theologians properly corresponds to classic
federal theology. Yet, as O. P. Robertson noted, "Virtually
every school of biblical interpretation today has come to
appreciate the significance of the covenants for the understanding of the distinctive message of the Scriptures."[10]

Challenges to Covenant Theology
from the Federal Vision

One of the more prominent challenges in confessional
circles to classic federalism in recent years has emerged
among a group that, interestingly, self-identified as proponents of a "Federal Vision" (FV). Although these
FV advocates argue for a revitalization of "the doctrine
of the covenant" (usually put this way instead of a doctrine "of covenant" or "of the covenants") and of the
church, the churches in NAPARC have, through a variety of study committees, determined that the FV is a
departure from classic federalism.[11] The views of the FV
proponents have not sprung full-blown as Athena from

---

10. O. P. Robertson, *The Christ of the Covenants* (Phillipsburg,
N.J.: P&R Publishing, 1987), vii.

11. Much of what follows derives from the Federal Vision section

the head of Zeus but rather have been in development for some time and involve issues about which the church has conversed down through the centuries. The historic roots of this controversy, one might argue, extend back even to the apostolic and ancient church.

Although it is true, for instance, that the bi-covenantalism (covenant of works and covenant of grace) and tri-covenantalism (covenant of redemption, additionally) of classic federal theology were not developed until the late sixteenth and early seventeenth centuries, many of the concerns addressed by the development of the covenant of works were present not only in Augustine's work on the fourfold state of man but also hinted at in the writings of Justin Martyr, Irenaeus, Athanasius, and others.[12] Obviously, supporters of classic federal theology would also maintain that it finds its true genesis in the Scriptures of the Old and New Testaments (and also, as some have noted, the intertestamental literature; cf. Sirach 17:1, 11–12). So the FV supporters need to be cognizant that if they wish, for example, to contend against a "judicial" theology, they do so not only against those who would affirm the covenant of works but also against Augustine and, to a lesser degree, Tertullian, Chrysostom, and a host of others (including rabbis before the Second Temple's destruction) in the ancient and medieval church. In other words, what was developed in federal theology was not a

---

of the OPC's *Report of the Committee*, 116–19, of which I was the primary author.

12. As noted in chapter 2 of this work.

novelty of the seventeenth century but was always present in at least seed form in historical theology, being rooted in the Scriptures (even also, as we have argued, with active obedience).[13]

Additionally, numerous scholars have also recognized that many of the tenets of federal theology may be found in incipient form in Zwingli, Bullinger, and even Calvin. This is important to note because some of the FV men claim to be returning to the nascent federalism of Bullinger and Calvin, as if these Reformers were at odds with or significantly differed from the "scholastic" federal theology that developed in the seventeenth century.[14] Thus, some FV proponents make a similar mistake to Perry Miller or Karl Barth in pitting Calvin against his followers. Those who would oppose both Bullinger to Beza and Calvin to the Calvinists of the next century have been ably refuted, as seen earlier, by Muller, Venema, Beach, and others. While there were certainly some different emphases, it is unwise and unwarranted to pit Calvin against the Westminster Confession as Perry Miller and a host of earlier scholars had done, although the tide now runs distinctly in the opposite direction.

---

13. For some of the background, see the articles on covenant and federal theology in John McClintock and James Strong, *Cyclopedia of Biblical, Theological and Ecclesiastical Literature* (1867–1887; repr., Grand Rapids: Baker, 1981). See also Hans J. Hillerbrand, ed., *The Oxford Encyclopedia of the Reformation* (New York: Oxford University Press, 1996), 1:442–45.

14. Richard Muller, "Reformed Confessions and Catechisms," in Hart, *Dictionary of Historical Theology*, 466–85.

Positive and Negative Influences of FV Theology

We must candidly admit that FV promoters are not alone among Reformed theologians, particularly of more recent times, in finding fault with classic federal theology. In the last century especially, several leading confessional Reformed theologians regarded classic federal theology as scholastic, rationalistic, and speculative. One may cite not only Barth and his many followers as those critical of federal theology but also more orthodox men like Herman Hoeksema, Klaas Schilder, and John Murray.[15]

Hoeksema rejected the covenant of works but, contra the FV partisans, also rejected any conditionality in the covenant of grace. He tended to read the covenant through election. Schilder, however, while taking a cautious approach to the covenant of works (sharply rejecting any notion of condign merit for prelapsarian Adam, for instance), emphasized the conditionality of the covenant and tended to view election from the perspective of the

---

15. Herman Hoeksema's *The Covenant: God's Tabernacle with Men* (repr., Grand Rapids: Reformed Free Publishing Association, 1973) serves as a concise statement of his conception of covenant. Schilder's position may be gathered from a speech he gave in the Netherlands in 1944, "The Main Points of the Doctrine of the Covenant" (private reprint, Canada, 1992) and from a work on the liberation of the Gereformeerde Kerken from the Synodical Churches (J. Kamphuis, *An Everlasting Covenant* [Launceston, Tasmania: Publication Organization of the Free Reformed Churches of Australia, 1985]). Murray's position on the covenant is set forth in *The Covenant of Grace* (London: Tyndale Press, 1954); and John Murray, "The Adamic Administration," in *Collected Writings of John Murray*, vol. 2, *Select Lectures in Systematic Theology* (Edinburgh: Banner of Truth, 1977), 47–59.

covenant. At about the same time in the mid-twentieth century, Murray argued for a recasting of covenant theology, seeing the covenant as purely an expression of God's unmerited favor to fallen man and thus not inaugurated until the postlapsarian situation. If Hoeksema emphasized *pactum salutis* above all and Schilder *historia salutis* (even as members of the Netherlands Reformed Congregations, for instance, stress *ordo salutis*), perhaps Murray's genius, however he might have erred in terms of classic federalism, was not to jettison one of these in favor of the others but to hold to the eternal, redemptive-historical, and experiential aspects of the salvation that is ours and is all of grace.

Of the FV men, some claim to be following in Schilder's footsteps[16] while others claim to be carrying on Murray's recasting of covenant theology (as does Norman Shepherd).[17] Hoeksema is lauded by FV supporters for rejecting the covenant of works,[18] but his decretal theology, even as is the experimental Calvinism of so many of

---

16. John Barach, "Covenant and Election," in *Federal Vision*, ed. Steve Wilkins and Duane Garner (Monroe, La.: Athanasius Press, 2004), 15.

17. James Jordan, "Merit versus Maturity: What Did Jesus Do for Us?" in Wilkins and Garner, *Federal Vision*, 151–55.

18. P. Andrew Sandlin, "Covenant in Redemptive History: 'Gospel and Law' or 'Trust and Obey,'" in Sandlin, *Backbone of the Bible*, 68. Sandlin cites in support Hoeksema's *Reformed Dogmatics* (Grand Rapids: Reformed Free Publishing Association, 1966), 214–26, and also Ralph Smith, *Eternal Covenant* (Moscow, Idaho: Canon Press, 2003), 61–83.

the Reformed and Puritan theologians, is quite out of step with the program of the Federal Vision. As a side note, one might add that many of the FV men also seem to be reacting against certain Reformed theologians as if these theologians represented most of those who hold to the classic federal theology as expressed in the Westminster Standards. For instance, Meredith Kline's view that one ought not to speak of grace in the prelapsarian context, arguing that grace should be defined exclusively as de-merited favor and thus applicable only in a fallen context (whether as common or special grace), is arguably a minority report within historic federal theology.[19] Francis Turretin better captures the mainstream position in his asserting that one may rightly speak of grace in the prelapsarian state and that there was a disproportion between Adam's obedience and the reward that would have followed, there thus being more than strict justice in view during the prelapsarian administration of the covenant of works.[20]

It is worth noting that while many of Kline's detractors regard him as viewing Adam as being capable of condign merit, his supporters claim that Kline believed only in Adamic merit *ex pacto*.[21] Similar to the tendency

---

19. Kline's view is ably set forth by a supporter and is fairly contrasted with Murray's (particularly in the latter's scrupling at the covenant of works while affirming Adamic federal headship) in Jeong Koo Jeon's *Covenant Theology* (Lanham, Md.: University Press of America, 1999).

20. Turretin, *Institutes of Elenctic Theology*, 1:574–78.

21. For a particularly interesting and insightful look at "two ways

of FV men to paint Kline as *the* representative of classic federal theology, FV promoters attack the view that faith consists of "assent alone" and seem to think that many hold to such a view, whereas Gordon Clark himself, as a modern proponent of the view that faith is intellectual assent to a proposition, lamented that most of the Reformed regarded faith as involving not only *notitia* and *assensus* but also *fiducia*.[22]

In addition to the influence of Schilder, Murray, and others of a more biblical and confessional bent, some of the men who support the Federal Vision have also been influenced by what has come to be called the New Perspective on Paul (NPP). Promoters of the NPP like Krister Stendahl, E. P. Sanders, James D. G. Dunn, and N. T. Wright have been quite influential in the last half century. Their position, often referred to as covenantal nomism, is that the Reformers, and Luther particularly, misread Paul through the lens of their own sixteenth-century concerns as if the errors of the Roman church were what Paul was dealing with in his battle against the Judaizers. According to the NPP, Paul, when he spoke of justification, was not so much concerned to teach about justification along the lines that Luther came to understand it, but to set forth the way that the Gentiles might be brought into the covenant

---

of reading Kline" on a related but different matter (the republication of the covenant of works in the Mosaic covenant), see the "Report of the Committee to Study Republication," 397–444.

22. Gordon H. Clark, *What Is Saving Faith?* (repr., Unicoi, Tenn.: Trinity Foundation, 2004), 82–88.

without having first to become Jews. Thus, justification in Paul was about how one gets into covenant, reduced to inclusion of the Gentiles. Numerous critics have noted that the position of covenantal nomism appears to be that one gets into the covenant by grace and stays in by works. This has been ably described and critiqued elsewhere by Venema, Gaffin, and Waters, among others.[23]

I believe that what we crucially need in this hour is not the Reformed revisionism of Miller, Barth, Federal Vision, the New Perspective on Paul, or the like. I believe we need a recovery of the hearty and balanced federal theology that we find embodied in the Westminster Standards and that remains, but for a few relatively minor alterations (certainly nothing impacting the system of doctrine contained therein), the confession and catechisms of the confessional Presbyterian churches here and elsewhere, notably, thinking in terms of the successors of the mainstream of the Church of Scotland, the Orthodox Presbyterian Church and the Presbyterian Church in America.

---

23. See the OPC's *Report of the Committee*, 71–109.

8

The Place of Active Obedience
in Confessional Interpretation

In addition to all the foregoing considerations, it might be
helpful to address questions of constitutional interpretation as they pertain to the affirmation of active obedience.
It is a commonplace in interpreting and applying constitutional law—whether the Westminster Confession as
part of the constitution of a Presbyterian church or the
U.S. Constitution as part of American jurisprudence—
that the interpretive process involves attention to the
original intent of the bodies that drafted and adopted the
particular laws at issue as well as the words themselves
contained in the laws. As noted in the OPC "Report of
the Committee on Creation Views,"

> In ecclesiastical law, as in all constitutional law, judi-
> catories that interpret the constitution should pay
> the most careful attention to the words of the con-
> stitution itself. The words drafted and adopted by
> the framers serve as the form of unity and bind the
> church together in its doctrine. The interpretation
> that the church as a whole has of the constitution
> has come to be referred to by the technical term

animus imponentis (which term is more fully defined below). The *animus* of the church, however, is shaped not only by the words of the constitution itself but also by the church studying and giving heed to what the original intent of those who framed the confession or its amendments was (among other things). Original intent, like *animus imponentis*, is also a technical term and refers to what the framers of a document, whether it is a civil or ecclesiastical constitution, had in mind when they wrote and adopted the constitution.[1]

In short, *original intent* denotes what the body that drafted the constitutional document(s) in question meant in adopting the particular language that it did. This term is preferred over *authorial intent*, since most constitutional documents are drafted and adopted by deliberative assemblies of some sort. The Westminster Assembly of Divines was certainly a deliberative body. The question then becomes how the original intent of the Westminster divines on any given issue is to be ascertained. Of course, in reading the confession and catechisms, a primary emphasis must always be placed on the words themselves: What do these particular words mean? But the words are not to be read out of context, and the concern for original intent always considers that a reading of any particular

---

1. *Minutes of the Seventy-First General Assembly of the Orthodox Presbyterian Church* (Willow Grove, Pa.: Orthodox Presbyterian Church, 2004), 257–58. I was the primary author of this section of the OPC's *Report of the Committee.*

part of the confession or catechisms should be in line with the intention of those who first wrote the words.

There are numerous ways that one might ascertain the original intent of the members of the Assembly: through writings of the divines (sermons, treatises, letters, etc.), through the minutes of the Assembly, through journals (like Lightfoot's), and through observations of contemporaries about the work of the Assembly. Original intent and a reading of the words at face value are never opposed to one another in sound constitutional interpretation. Rather, original intent simply helps provide the proper *Sitz im Leben* in which to read the text in a fashion that is not decontextualized but faithful to the meaning of those who wrote and adopted it.

Animus Imponentis

Original intent, however, is not the only matter of concern in constitutional interpretation: *animus imponentis* is also at issue. *Animus imponentis* (the intention of the imposing body) means that not only the original intent of the framers of the Westminster Assembly (or of the framers of any subsequent amendments) is to be considered in our ecclesiastical assemblies but also the way in which those assemblies themselves understand the constitution. This is particularly relevant when dealing with the Westminster Standards since they were not the product of an ecclesiastical judicatory but were instead the product of a body that was advisory to English Parliament. As such, the intention of the Scottish church in adopting the Westminster Standards (in 1649) is, for that church, as important (if not more so) as the intention of the Assembly.[2] Similarly, then, the *animus imponentis* is significant for the Presbyterian Church in the colonies when it passed the Adopting Act of 1729 or when the OPC adopted the form of the Westminster Standards that it did at the second General Assembly of the OPC in November 1936. Some might even regard such adopting acts by ecclesiastical judicatories as savoring more of an original intent situation than an *animus imponentis* one. Regardless of which is correct, the point remains that in confessional hermeneutics, significant consideration must be given to acts of church judicatories subsequent to the adoption of the Westminster Standards.

Original Intent at Westminster

What was the original intent of the Assembly in regard to the question of affirming active obedience? This has been the main focus of this work. One might argue (as I have

---

2. McKay, "Scotland and the Westminster Assembly," 1:240–41. The Scottish General Assembly did make two qualifications (having to do with ecclesiastical officers and assemblies and the power of civil magistrates to call such), the point here being that the WCF bore authority in the Scottish church only when and as that church adopted it as her confession. So too with the American church in 1729 and 1788/89 (at the first General Assembly) and following, as particular Presbyterian denominations had occasion to come into being (for which, see D. G. Hart and John R. Muether, *Seeking a Better Country: 300 Years of American Presbyterianism* (Phillipsburg, N.J.: P&R Publishing, 2007).

herein) that when the question was directly engaged, the Assembly affirmed active obedience (in 1643) and never subsequently modified its position but reaffirmed it in several important places throughout the confession and catechisms. Even if, however, as some speculate, the Westminster Assembly "pulled its punches" in 1645–1646 by not using the word *whole* in chapter 11 (on justification) in the WCF, such a position takes only original intent into account. But *animus imponentis* must also be taken into account, particularly when we consider that the Westminster Standards are to operate as constitutional documents within our judicatories, serving as the doctrinal standards to which Presbyterian churches bind themselves and to which they hold their office bearers doctrinally accountable. How have the churches that have adopted the Westminster Standards as part of their own constitutions understood the issue of the affirmation of active obedience? Does the Scottish church, or the OPC, or the PCA read the standards to affirm active obedience? How is such to be gathered? How are we, in other words, to ascertain what the mind of the imposing body—the Presbyterian churches of which we are a part and in which many of us serve as office bearers—is regarding active obedience?

Animus Imponentis after Westminster

Part of what may go into the formation of the church's *animus imponentis* is the work of her leading theologians. It is the case that the theological works that have been perhaps

the most formative in the Presbyterian Church (such as
the systematic theologies of Francis Turretin in the seventeenth century and Charles Hodge in the nineteenth
century)[3] have strongly affirmed active obedience, as did
James Buchanan in his lectures in nineteenth-century
Scotland and a dying J. Gresham Machen (helping shape
the animus of the OPC).[4] By itself, this is not decisive, of
course. These theologians are not the standards. It is not
until recent times, however, that any noted confessional
theologians have departed from an affirmation of active
obedience, apart from the earlier demurral of Piscator and
others, along with certain Westminster divines.[5]

More decisive would be testimonies (as in the Scottish tradition) or study committee reports about the
matter. The latter have not been produced until recently,
and it is widely known that both the PCA and OPC
committees that addressed the broader question of justification affirmed active obedience. A judicial case would
be a helpful part of gathering the church's animus on the
matter, but I am aware of no judicial cases in the history of Presbyterianism (with the possible exception of
some recent cases in the PCA more broadly directed at
Federal Vision) that have directly deliberated whether the
accused affirms active obedience.[6]

---

3. Cited in the preface of this work.

4. Buchanan, *Doctrine of Justification*. See the preface of this work
for Machen's view.

5. As noted in the previous chapter of this work.

6. I know of no such case in the history of the Reformed and

A parallel example might help us with this active obedience case. In recent years it has become evident to careful students of the Westminster Assembly that a few divines at Westminster had sympathy for Amyraldianism, which is to say that a few divines might have been "four-point Calvinists," unwilling to affirm definite (limited) atonement, preferring a hypothetical universalism instead. Several scholars have reflected on how this might have impacted some of the debates and have noted that, unlike the Synod of Dort, the Westminster Assembly did not affirm limited atonement in explicit terms. This is not to suggest that the Assembly adopted any expressions that would in any way mitigate against limited atonement or that the work of the Assembly, taken in the integrity of its whole expression, failed to affirm the essentials of this doctrine. It is simply to say that the Westminster Standards arguably lack an explicit statement affirming limited atonement.

Although the Assembly might have slightly pulled its punches on the issue of limited atonement, few if any presbyters in our confessional Presbyterian churches would permit someone who denied limited atonement to

---

Presbyterian churches, apart from the early seventeenth-century condemnation of Piscator and others. The caveat of the "possible exception of some recent cases in the PCA" appears above, chiefly because of the trial of Peter Leithart in the PCA by the Presbytery of the Northwest. Much more was at issue in that case than the matter of active obedience (Leithart was not convicted of the charges brought against him), and the PCA rather decidedly upheld active obedience in its report on justification, as did the OPC in its report.

be a minister in our churches. Here is a clear case in which not simply original intent is at issue but also *animus imponentis*.[7] Judicatories in both the PCA and OPC read the Westminster Standards in a way that requires the affirmation of limited atonement, even though the original intent may not be perfectly clear on the matter. Similarly, the recent reports of committees erected by such bodies also testify that an animus has developed in the church that reads our standards to require the affirmation of active obedience, even as they routinely require the affirmation of the doctrine of limited atonement.

Conclusion

Three things seem to be missed by those who contend that, since the Westminster Assembly did not in 1645–1646 affirm active obedience the way that it did in 1643, the church cannot, without amending those symbols, require her office bearers to affirm active obedience.

First, simply because the specific language used early in the Assembly to affirm active obedience was not repeated in what we now call the Westminster Standards does not mean that the Assembly did not continue to affirm active obedience. As has been argued extensively herein,

---

7. In "The Days of Creation and Confession Subscription in the OPC," *Westminster Theological Journal* 63 (2001): 235–49, J. V. Fesko argues along similar lines, contending that we must take proper account of the *animus imponentis* at a number of key points in our constitutional interpretation, although he tends to pit it against original intent at times, which I do not find the most careful use of the concept.

the standards contain numerous expressions that support the doctrine of the imputation of the active obedience of Christ in our justification.

Second, the Assembly was not a court of the church and did not have the power in itself to exclude any of her members who differed from her, as do our church courts. It should not be inferred from Thomas Gataker's continuation at Westminster that the Assembly backed off its earlier affirmation of active obedience, enabling someone like Gataker to continue to serve. It is unwarranted to think that if the Assembly had not backed off of its support of active obedience, that it would have excluded Gataker from service. This is not to suggest that the Assembly was impotent: as empowered by Parliament, the Assembly did examine ministerial candidates and academics, deal with suspected heretics, and perform other ecclesiastical functions.[8] But it remained the creature of Parliament in an Erastian church. Twisse, Gataker, and Vines, differing as they did from the majority who clearly affirmed active obedience in 1643, were not thereafter excluded from the Assembly (as the Arminians were from Dort in 1618 or the Arians from Nicaea in 325), not because they necessarily came to agree with the Westminster Assembly but because Parliament permitted them and others like them to continue to serve.

---

8. Chad Van Dixhoorn deals with these matters in a number of his works, including one of his more recent books, *God's Ambassadors: The Westminster Assembly and the Reformation of the English Pulpit, 1643–1653* (Grand Rapids: Reformation Heritage Books, 2017), 41–61.

Third, even if the Westminster Standards could be shown to allow for a denial of active obedience, it is not necessarily the case that present-day deniers would stop at a mere denial of active obedience; they would likely have problems with the whole theological scheme of Westminster, of which active obedience is merely an important plank. It needs to be noted that one cannot simply pluck a position from a sound writer and do something entirely different with it. Norman Shepherd and James Jordan, for example, both deny the covenant of works and cite John Murray in defense of such a denial.[9] While Murray denied the covenant of works as such, affirming the "Adamic administration" instead, his denial does not amount to the same thing as a monocovenantalism that fails properly to distinguish the dynamics of the prefall and postfall world, mixing law and gospel.

All this is to say that even if one remains convinced that the Westminster Assembly failed to affirm active obedience, the schema put forward by Shepherd, Jordan, and others does not track with the Westminster Standards. They are doing theology on a different trajectory than the sort of covenantal theology found in the Westminster Standards. The church, after all, in ascertaining the original intent of the drafters and/or adopters of her doctrinal standards and in expressing her *animus* thereupon, polices her own standards and has properly concluded that those who deny active obedience are wanting as Reformed

---

9. See the OPC's *Report of the Committee*, 117–18.

theologians.[10] I would urge that the church is warranted in such a conclusion: no case can effectively be made that the Westminster Assembly failed to affirm finally the imputation of the active obedience of Christ in our justification; the Assembly initially embraced active obedience and retained that conviction throughout its work.

---

10. The OPC, PCA, RCUS, OCRC, URCNA, and RPCNA have either condemned FV and NPP errors or have adopted statements that reaffirm and highlight confessional statements that militate against positions of at least some of their supporters. Several seminaries also have adopted statements opposing these errors, the fullest being that of Mid-America Reformed Seminary, *Doctrinal Testimony Regarding Recent Errors* (Dyer, Ind.: Mid-America Reformed Seminary, 2007).

Bibliography

Anselm. *Why God Became Man.* In *Anselm of Canterbury, The Major Works.* New York: Oxford University Press, 1998.

Barach, John. "Covenant and Election." In *Federal Vision.* Edited by Steve Wilkins and Duane Garner. Monroe, La.: Athanasius Press, 2004.

Barker, William. *Puritan Profiles: 54 Puritan Personalities Drawn Together by the Westminster Assembly.* Fearn, Scotland: Mentor, 1996.

Bavinck, Herman. *Reformed Dogmatics.* Vol. 3, *Sin and Salvation in Christ.* Edited by John Bolt. Translated by John Vriend. Grand Rapids: Baker Academic, 2006.

Beach, J. Mark. *Christ and the Covenant: Francis Turretin's Federal Theology as a Defense of the Doctrine of Grace.* Göttingen: Vandenhoeck & Ruprecht, 2007.

Bierma, Lyle D. "Federal Theology in the Sixteenth Century: Two Traditions." *Westminster Theological Journal* 44, no. 2 (Fall 1983): 304–21.

Boersma, H. *A Hot Pepper Corn: Richard Baxter's Doctrine of Justification.* Zoetermeer: Boekencentrum, 1993.

Buchanan, James. *The Doctrine of Justification: An Outline of Its History in the Church and of Its Exposition from*

Scripture. Reprint, Pelham, Ala.: Solid Ground Christian Books, 2004.

Calvin, John. *Institutes of the Christian Religion*. Edited by John T. McNeill. Translated by Ford Lewis Battles. Library of Christian Classics. 1559. Reprint, Philadelphia: Westminster Press, 1960.

Carruthers, S. W. *The Everyday Work of the Westminster Assembly*. Edited by J. Ligon Duncan III. Reprint, Greenville, S.C.: Reformed Academic Press, 1994.

Chemnitz, Martin. *Examination of the Council of Trent*. Reprint, St. Louis: Concordia, 1971.

Clark, Gordon H. *What Is Saving Faith?* Reprint, Unicoi, Tenn.: Trinity Foundation, 2004.

Clark, R. Scott. "Do This and Live: Christ's Active Obedience as the Ground of Justification." In *Covenant, Justification, and Pastoral Ministry: Essays by the Faculty of Westminster Seminary California*. Edited by R. Scott Clark. Phillipsburg, N.J.: P&R Publishing, 2007.

Como, David R. *Blown by the Spirit: Puritanism and the Emergence of an Antinomian Underground in Pre-Civil-War England*. Stanford, Calif.: Stanford University Press, 2004.

de Campos, Heber Carlos, Jr. *Doctrine in Development: Johannes Piscator and Debates over Christ's Active Obedience*. Grand Rapids: Reformation Heritage Books, 2017.

———. "Johannes Piscator (1546–1625) and the Consequent Development of the Imputation of Christ's Active Obedience." PhD diss., Calvin Theological Seminary, 2008.

Duncan, J. Ligon. "Recent Objections to Covenant Theology: A Description, Evaluation, and Response." In *The Westminster Confession into the 21st Century*. 3 vols. Edited by L. Duncan. Fearn, Scotland: Mentor, 2004.

Ferguson, Sinclair. *The Holy Spirit*. Downers Grove, Ill.: InterVarsity Press, 1996.

———. "Westminster Assembly." In *The Dictionary of Scottish Church History and Theology*. Downers Grove, Ill.: InterVarsity Press, 1993.

———. *The Whole Christ: Legalism, Antinomianism, and Gospel Assurance—Why the Marrow Controversy Still Matters*. Wheaton, Ill.: Crossway, 2016.

Fesko, J. V. "The Days of Creation and Confession Subscription in the OPC." *Westminster Theological Journal* 63 (2001): 235–49.

———. *Justification: Understanding the Classic Reformed Doctrine*. Phillipsburg, N.J.: P&R Publishing, 2008.

———. *The Theology of the Westminster Standards: Historical Context and Theological Insights*. Wheaton, Ill.: Crossway, 2014.

———. "The Westminster Confession and Lapsarianism: Calvin and the Divines." In Duncan, *Westminster Confession into the 21st Century*, 2:477–525.

Gamble, Richard C. "Current Trends in Calvin Research, 1982–90." In *Calvinus Sacrae Scripturae Professor*, edited by Wilhelm H. Neuser, 91–112. Grand Rapids: Eerdmans, 1994.

Gamble, Whitney G. *Christ and the Law: Antinomianism at*

the Westminster Assembly. Grand Rapids: Reformation Heritage Books, 2018.

Gataker, Thomas. *An Antidote against Errour, concerning Justification.* London: Henry Brome, 1670.

Gathercole, Simon. *Defending Substitution: An Essay on Atonement in Paul.* Grand Rapids: Baker Academic, 2015.

Grillmeier, Aloys. *Christ in Christian Tradition.* Translated by John Bowden. 2nd ed. Atlanta: John Knox Press, 1975.

Hart, D. G., and John R. Muether. *Seeking a Better Country: 300 Years of American Presbyterianism.* Phillipsburg, N.J.: P&R Publishing, 2007.

Hart, Trevor A., and Richard Bauckham. *The Dictionary of Historical Theology.* Grand Rapids: Eerdmans, 2000.

Hillerbrand, Hans J., ed. *The Oxford Encyclopedia of the Reformation.* New York: Oxford University Press, 1996.

Hodge, Charles. *Systematic Theology.* 3 vols. New York: Scribner, Armstrong, and Company, 1871.

Hoeksema, Herman. *The Covenant: God's Tabernacle with Men.* Reprint, Grand Rapids: Reformed Free Publishing Association, 1973.

———. *Reformed Dogmatics.* Grand Rapids: Reformed Free Publishing Association, 1966.

Jeon, Jeong Koo. *Covenant Theology.* Lanham, Md.: University Press of America, 1999.

Jones, Mark. *Antinomianism: Reformed Theology's Unwelcome Guest.* Phillipsburg, N.J.: P&R Publishing, 2013.

Jordan, James. "Merit versus Maturity: What Did Jesus Do for Us?" In *Federal Vision,* edited by Steve Wilkins and Duane Garner, 151–55. Monroe, La.: Athanasius Press, 2004.

Jue, Jeffrey. "Active Obedience of Christ and the Theology of the Westminster Standards: A Historical Investigation." In *Justified in Christ: God's Plan for Us in Justification*, edited by K. Scott Oliphint, 99–130. Fearn, Scotland: Mentor, 2007.

Kamphuis, J. *An Everlasting Covenant*. Launceston, Tasmania: Publication Organization of the Free Reformed Churches of Australia, 1985.

Kirk, Daniel. "The Sufficiency of the Cross (I): The Crucifixion as Jesus' Act of Obedience." *Scottish Bulletin of Evangelical Theology* 24, no. 1 (Spring 2006): 36–64.

———. "The Sufficiency of the Cross (II): The Law, the Cross, and Justification." *Scottish Bulletin of Evangelical Theology* 24, no. 2 (Autumn 2006): 133–54.

Kolb, Robert. "Human Performance and the Righteousness of Faith: Martin Chemnitz's Anti-Roman Polemic in Formula of Concord III." In *By Faith Alone: Essays on Justification in Honor of Gerhard O. Forde*, edited by Joseph A. Burgess and Marc Kolden, 125–39. Grand Rapids: Eerdmans, 2004.

Lehrer, Steve, and Jeff Volker. "Examining the Imputation of Active Obedience of Christ: A Study in Calvinistic Sacred Cow-ism." Accessed at http://idsaudio.org /ids/pdf/classic/imputation.pdf.

Letham, Robert. *Through Western Eyes: Eastern Orthodoxy; A Reformed Perspective*. Fearn, Scotland: Mentor, 2007.

———. *Westminster Assembly: Reading Its Theology in*

Historical Context. Phillipsburg, N.J.: P&R Publishing, 2009.

———. *The Work of Christ.* Downers Grove, Ill.: Inter Varsity Press, 1993.

Lillback, Peter. *The Binding of God: Calvin's Role in the Development of Covenant Theology.* Grand Rapids: Baker Academic, 2001.

Luther, Martin. "Instructions to the Perplexed and Doubting, To George Spenlein, April 8, 1516." In *Luther: Letters of Spiritual Counsel.* Vancouver, British Columbia: Regent College Publishing, 2003.

Lynn, William D. *Christ's Redemptive Merit: The Nature of Its Causality according to St. Thomas.* Rome: Gregorian University Press, 1962.

Machen, J. Gresham. "Active Obedience of Christ." In *God Transcendent and Other Selected Sermons,* 172–80. Grand Rapids: Eerdmans, 1949.

McClintock, John, and James Strong. *Cyclopedia of Biblical, Theological and Ecclesiastical Literature.* 1867–1887. Reprint, Grand Rapids: Baker, 1981.

McKay, W. D. J. "Scotland and the Westminster Assembly." In Duncan, *Westminster Confession into the 21st Century,* 1:213–45.

Melanchthon, Philipp. *Loci Communes.* Translated by Clyde L. Manschreck. Grand Rapids: Baker, 1965.

Mid-America Reformed Seminary. *Doctrinal Testimony Regarding Recent Errors.* Dyer, Ind.: Mid-America Reformed Seminary, 2007.

Mitchell, Alex F. *The Westminster Assembly: Its History and*

        Standards. 1883. Reprint, Edmonton, Alberta: Still Water Revival Books, 1992.

Mitchell, Alex F., and John Struthers. *Minutes of the Sessions of the Assembly of Divines.* Edinburgh: William Blackwood and Sons, 1874.

Muller, Richard. *After Calvin: Studies in the Development of a Theological Tradition.* New York: Oxford University Press, 1993.

———. "Directions in Current Calvin Research." *Religious Studies Review* 27, no. 2 (2002): 131–38.

———. "Reformed Confessions and Catechisms." In Hart, *Dictionary of Historical Theology,* 466–85.

Murray, John. "The Adamic Administration." In *Collected Writings of John Murray.* Vol. 2, *Select Lectures in Systematic Theology.* Edinburgh: Banner of Truth, 1977.

———. *The Covenant of Grace.* London: Tyndale Press, 1954.

———. *Redemption Accomplished and Applied.* Grand Rapids: Eerdmans, 1955.

Niesel, Wilhelm. *The Theology of Calvin.* Philadelphia: Westminster Press, 1956.

Norris, R. M. "The Thirty-Nine Articles at the Westminster Assembly." PhD diss., University of St. Andrews, 1977.

Oberman, Heiko. *The Harvest of Medieval Theology: Gabriel Biel and Late Medieval Nominalism.* Grand Rapids: Baker Academic, 2000.

Oliphint, K. Scott, ed. *Justified in Christ: God's Plan for Us in Justification.* Fearn, Scotland: Christian Focus, 2007.

Orthodox Presbyterian Church. *Minutes of the Seventy-First General Assembly of the Orthodox Presbyterian Church*. Willow Grove, Pa.: Orthodox Presbyterian Church, 2004.

———. "The Report of the Committee to Study Republication of the General Assembly of the Orthodox Presbyterian Church." In *Minutes of the 83rd General Assembly of the Orthodox Presbyterian Church*. 2016.

———. *Report of the Committee to Study the Doctrine of Justification*. Willow Grove, Pa.: Committee on Christian Education of the Orthodox Presbyterian Church, 2007.

Owen, John. *The Doctrine of Justification by Faith*. Grand Rapids: Reformation Heritage Books, 2009.

Parnham, David. "The Covenantal Quietism of Tobias Crisp." *Church History* 75, no. 3 (September 2006): 511–43.

———. *Heretics Within: Anthony Wotten, John Goodwin, and the Orthodox Divines*. Brighton, UK: Sussex Academic Press, 2014.

———. "Motions of Law and Grace: The Puritan in the Antinomian." *Westminster Theological Journal* 70 (2008): 73–104.

Patterson, W. B. *King James VI and I and the Reunion of Christendom*. New York: Cambridge University Press, 1997.

Paul, Robert S. *The Assembly of the Lord: Politics and Religion in the Westminster Assembly and the "Grand Debate."* Edinburgh: T&T Clark, 1985.

Pelikan, Jaroslav. *The Christian Tradition: A History of the Development of Doctrine.* Vol. 1, *The Emergence of the Catholic Tradition (100–600).* Chicago: University of Chicago Press, 1971.

———. *The Christian Tradition: A History of the Development of Doctrine.* Vol. 2, *The Spirit of Eastern Christendom.* Chicago: University of Chicago Press, 1974.

Pelikan, Jaroslav, ed. *Creeds and Confessions of Faith in the Christian Tradition.* New Haven, Conn.: Yale University Press, 2003.

Pelikan, Jaroslav, and Valerie Hotchkiss, eds. *Creeds and Confessions of Faith in the Christian Tradition.* New Haven, Conn.: Yale University Press, 2003.

Piper, John. *Counted Righteous in Christ: Should We Abandon the Imputation of Christ's Righteousness?* Wheaton, Ill.: Crossway, 2002.

Robertson, O. P. *The Christ of the Covenants.* Phillipsburg, N.J.: P&R Publishing, 1987.

Sandlin, P. Andrew. "Covenant in Redemptive History: 'Gospel and Law' or 'Trust and Obey.'" In *Backbone of the Bible: Covenant in Contemporary Perspective,* edited by P. Andrew Sandlin, 63–84. Nacogdoches, Tex.: Covenant Media Press, 2004.

Schaff, Philip, ed. *The Creeds of Christendom.* Reprint, Grand Rapids: Baker, 1985.

Schilder, Klaas. "The Main Points of the Doctrine of the Covenant." Private reprint, Canada, 1992.

Shepherd, Norman. "The Imputation of Active Obedience." In *A Faith That Is Never Alone: A Response to Westminster Seminary California,* edited by P. Andrew

Sandlin, 249–78. LaGrange, Calif.: Kerygma Press, 2007.

———. "Justification by Works in Reformed Theology." In Sandlin, *Backbone of the Bible*, 103–20.

Smith, Ralph. *Eternal Covenant*. Moscow, Idaho: Canon Press, 2003.

Southern, R. W. *Saint Anselm: A Portrait in a Landscape*. New York: Cambridge University Press, 1990.

Stewart, Kenneth. *Ten Myths about Calvinism: Recovering the Breadth of the Reformed Tradition*. Downers Grove, Ill.: InterVarsity Press, 2011.

Stonehouse, Ned B. *J. Gresham Machen: A Biographical Memoir*. 1954. Reprint, Willow Grove, Pa.: Committee for the Historian of the Orthodox Presbyterian Church, 2004.

Strange, Alan. "The Affirmation of the Imputation of the Active Obedience of Christ at the Westminster Assembly of Divines." *The Confessional Presbyterian* 4 (2008).

———. "The Imputation of the Active Obedience of Christ at the Westminster Assembly." In *Drawn into Controversie: Reformed Theological Diversity and Debates within Seventeenth-Century British Puritanism*, edited by Michael A. G. Haykin and Mark Jones, 31–51. Göttingen: Vandenhoeck & Ruprecht, 2011.

Tanner, Norman P., ed. *Decrees of the Ecumenical Councils*. Vol. 1, *Nicaea to Lateran V*. London and Washington, DC: Sheed and Ward / Georgetown University Press, 1990.

Turretin, Francis. *Institutes of Elenctic Theology*. Translated by George Musgrave Giger. Edited by James T. Dennison Jr. Phillipsburg, N.J.: P&R Publishing, 1992–1997.

Twisse, William. *The Riches of Gods Love unto the Vessells of Mercy, Consistent with His Absolute Hatred or Reprobation of the Vessells of Wrath...* Oxford: Printers to the University, 1653.

———. *Treatise concerning Predestination.* London: J. D. for Andrew Crook, 1646.

Van Dixhoorn, Chad. *God's Ambassadors: The Westminster Assembly and the Reformation of the English Pulpit, 1643–1653.* Grand Rapids: Reformation Heritage Books, 2017.

———. "Reforming the Reformation: Theological Debate at the Westminster Assembly, 1643–1652." PhD diss., University of Cambridge, 2004.

———. "The Strange Silence of Prolocutor Twisse: Predestination and Politics in the Westminster Assembly's Debate over Justification." *The Sixteenth Century Journal* 40 (2009): 395–418.

Van Dixhoorn, Chad, and David F. Wright, eds. *The Minutes and Papers of the Westminster Assembly, 1643–1653.* 5 vols. New York: Oxford University Press, 2012.

VanDrunen, David. "To Obey Is Better than Sacrifice: A Defense of Active Obedience of Christ the Light of Recent Criticism." In *By Faith Alone: Answering the Challenges to the Doctrine of Justification,* edited by Gary L. W. Johnson and Guy P. Waters, 127–46. Wheaton, Ill.: Crossway, 2007.

Venema, Cornelis. *Accepted and Renewed in Christ: The "Two-fold Grace of God" and the Interpretation of Calvin's*

Theology. Göttingen: Vandenhoeck & Ruprecht, 2007.

—————. "Calvin's Doctrine of the Imputation of Christ's Righteousness: Another Example of 'Calvin against the Calvinists'?" *Mid-America Journal of Theology* 20 (2009): 15–47.

—————. *Heinrich Bullinger and the Doctrine of Predestination: Author of "the Other Reformed Tradition."* Grand Rapids: Baker Academic, 2002.

Warfield, Benjamin B. "John Calvin the Theologian." In *Calvin and Augustine*. Edited by Samuel G. Craig. Philadelphia: Presbyterian and Reformed Publishing, 1971.

—————. *The Westminster Assembly and Its Work*. New York: Oxford University Press, 1931.

White, J. Wesley. "The Denial of the Imputation of the Active Obedience of Christ: Piscator on Justification." *Confessional Presbyterian* 3 (2007): 147–54.

—————. "Saying 'Justification by Faith Alone' Isn't Enough." *Mid-America Journal of Theology* 17 (2006): 256–66.

Scripture Index

Confessions Index